THE ETHICAL
TEACHING OF PAUL

THE ETHICAL TEACHING OF PAUL
A Study in Origin

By

MARY EDITH ANDREWS

ASSISTANT PROFESSOR OF RELIGION
GOUCHER COLLEGE

CHAPEL HILL
THE UNIVERSITY OF NORTH CAROLINA PRESS
1934

COPYRIGHT, 1934, BY
THE UNIVERSITY OF NORTH CAROLINA PRESS

PRINTED IN THE UNITED STATES OF AMERICA BY THE SEEMAN PRINTERY,
DURHAM, N. C., AND BOUND BY L. H. JENKINS, INC., RICHMOND, VA.

THIS BOOK WAS DIGITALLY PRINTED.

To My Mother

PREFACE

WHEN the ancient sage many years ago said, "Of making many books there is no end," he spoke more truly, perhaps, than he knew. His note of admonition has been so consistently disregarded that it requires no unusual temerity to add another volume to the extensive literature on Paul even as one remembers that to Koheleth "this, too, is vanity."

But if it is true that "the interpretation of Scripture has been an aspect of Christianity's adaptation to its environment," it is to be expected that with a rapidly changing intellectual scene new angles of approach will reveal results that were unimaginable a generation ago. It should not be a matter of surprise that modern New Testament scholarship should reflect the intellectual interests of its own day. The rise of the social sciences and of a new technique in the writing of history are only two of the contemporary intellectual interests which are being exhibited in the field of New Testament study.

The present volume is offered as a contribution to the study of Paul's letters parallel to that which has been in progress for more than a decade in the study of the Synoptic gospels. This study owes much to contemporary German scholarship, which first brought to light the current method of *Formgeschichte*, which has proved a useful tool in the investigation of Paul's letters, as it has been of value in the other field. It owes still more to the social-historical method best exemplified in the writings of Dean

Shirley Jackson Case and other members of the group of scholars to which he belongs. In fact, this volume may be regarded as a contribution to the "Studies in the History of New Testament Interpretation and Criticism," a research project of the Department of New Testament and Early Christian Literature of the University of Chicago.

To Dean Case and Professor Donald W. Riddle I would express my most sincere appreciation: to the former for helpful suggestions at the beginning of the study and in two seminars; to the latter for his unfailing interest and patience as well as for valuable counsel throughout both the preparation and the revision of the work. I am indebted also to my colleague, Professor Anna Irene Miller, who kindly read the whole manuscript, and to my friend, Mrs. Sarah R. Burke, who gave welcome aid in reading proof.

Acknowledgment is made to the *Journal of Religion* for permission to use certain material from my article, "The Problem of Motive in the Ethics of Paul," which has already appeared in its columns, and to G. P. Putnam's Sons and the Columbia University Press for privilege to quote from works for which they hold the copyright. I would also record my debt to the American Translation of the New Testament by Professor Edgar Johnson Goodspeed. Even though the passages quoted are my own translation from Souter's Greek New Testament, the discussions of Paul's thought reveal in every line the influence of the American Translation. The selected bibliography supplied for each chapter and the footnotes reveal still further my indebtedness to many others.

MARY E. ANDREWS

Goucher College
Baltimore

TABLE OF CONTENTS

CHAPTER	PAGE
PREFACE	vii
INTRODUCTION	3
I. AN ETHICAL PROBLEM: MUST GENTILES BECOME JEWS TO BE CHRISTIANS?	9
II. THE PERSONAL EQUATION IN CORINTH: A CONFLICT OF IDEALS	39
III. COMMUNITY PROBLEMS IN CORINTH: NORMS OF CONDUCT	69
IV. WAS PAUL AN INTELLECTUAL?	102
V. PAUL THE JEW	135
CONCLUSION	169
BIBLIOGRAPHY	176
INDEX	181

THE ETHICAL
TEACHING OF PAUL

INTRODUCTION

THE statement of Paul that he became all things to all men was nothing short of prophetic—in the predictive sense. He *has* become all things to all men. He has long been considered the earliest Christian theologian. Professor Deissmann first drew Paul out of the ranks of Christianity's great theologians and placed him among the world's great missionaries. Even Deissmann neglects one major interest of Paul the missionary —his concern with problems of human conduct. In fact, those who have studied Paul most exhaustively have not been interested in his ethical teaching. Interest in practical problems of human conduct, always of primary importance to Paul, has long been secondary to the matters of doctrinal and of speculative import. Only during the past generation have Paul's interpreters deigned to include even a chapter on the subject of his ethics, and even then they have made a purely theological approach. This common theological bias is revealed in the fact that an able contemporary New Testament scholar, after criticism of the approaches of the earlier rationalistic and idealistic theologians, proceeds to explain Paul's ethical outlook in terms of the theology of Karl Barth. Even modern theologians are sometimes found in glass houses after they have thrown stones.

A survey of the literature on the subject of Paul's ethics reveals the fact that Paul has been made to teach what is acceptable to his interpreters. His ethics has been described as "interim-ethics" by some, while that term has been repudiated by others. He is considered a great creative genius in the realm of ethics or he is said to be original only in his doctrine of justification by faith, which is regarded merely as a fighting point by two eminent men and as his central idea by a third and equally reputable scholar. He is sacramentarian, but he reinterprets the Hellenistic idea of sacrament, so that sacramental and ethical are not in contradiction. His mysticism roots in his Hellenism, in his eschatology, or in his communion with God, according as his different interpreters use data.

The present study is undertaken in the conviction that the time has come for a more human approach to the problem of Paul's ethical teaching. With first-hand sources at our disposal surely it is not necessary to exalt Paul's *ideas* at the expense of his *behavior*, to depict him as the theologian instead of as the missionary grappling with real problems of human need. Perhaps he is not so much the deep thinker, the intellectual, as the fiery propagandist of his faith; perhaps he deals more in word-pictures that convey meaning to his hearers than in abstruse theological speculation. Perhaps he is more at home in his first-century environment than in a modern one; and perhaps it would be more effective to see him in relation to his own problems than as an authority for the solution of ours.

While the ethical teaching of Paul has been neglected, some notable contributions have been made in related fields that have bearing upon the problem. The materials are available for a definitely social-historical approach to the ethical teaching of Paul. We have first-hand documents from his own pen, letters to at least four Christian communities in which he had worked and two other communities which he knew only through others. It is pos-

INTRODUCTION 5

sible to reconstruct the social situations that Paul faced as a missionary of the new faith. It is possible to analyze the life-situations of Christian groups as Paul's letters reveal them and as we are able through the results of competent research to understand the environment of early Christianity. The social approach builds upon tested methods of research. It utilizes the methods of literary and historical criticism, but it seeks to supplement both of these by insisting that the human experience in society is the matter of major moment.

Viewed from this angle the intensely practical nature of the problems of the Christian communities is at once apparent. There is little that is theoretical, except as Paul argues to defend his practices. To select a few examples: Must Gentiles first become Jews to be Christians? Must Christians observe the Law of Moses? The problem of marriage is a complicated one. The Christian community operates under pagan laws of marriage and divorce. What is to be done about the pagan couple one of whom becomes a Christian? What is the Christian position on divorce? How is the Christian to regard the adulterer? May Christians participate in pagan social and religious life? What place shall women have in the cult-meetings? How are these meetings to be conducted? Practical problems abound.

An analysis of the social situations which Paul faced should provide the surest norms for his motivation of conduct, a point at which the extant studies of the ethics of Paul are lamentably weak. When the question of the source of Paul's ethical incentive has been raised in the past, one answer has invariably come to the fore: scholars have long pointed to the fact of Paul's early training in the Jewish religion. Even the recent work of Professor

Enslin, certainly the most thorough and least theological treatment of Paul's ethics in English, arrives at this same conclusion. Paul's virtual independence of all environing factors except Judaism is stressed; yet there is no mention of Diaspora Judaism which was certainly the Judaism of Paul. To find that Paul's emphasis lies in "the mystical union of the believer in Christ and the resulting union of the brethren in Christ" is really not to find Judaism the predominant factor. It seems to the present writer that the stock answer that Paul was what he was in ethical outlook only because he was a Jew needs revision in the light of all the circumstances in the midst of which he found himself. It is an assumption that an inductive study of Paul's letters will not substantiate. It is an assumption that will be tested in the following pages.

In the analysis of Paul's letters to find the vital situations embodied in them, another fact of interest methodologically, at present not widely recognized, is apparent. In all the letters except those to the Corinthians are to be found sections of ethical precepts at the end of the letter. These sections are usually treated in the same manner as the rest of the letter for exegetical purposes. In one sense this is legitimate procedure because Paul's seal of approval is there. In another sense, however, they should be used with caution. They are so general in content even to the point of approaching the stereotyped that they may not be trusted for data on a given situation. They give the impression of previous formulation and use, not of free composition. To the student of the genesis of Paul's ethical teaching this distinction is important, for it at once lays open the question of the use of traditional material in the letters, which of course has direct bearing on the question of the genesis of the ethical teaching. A few German

INTRODUCTION 7

scholars have done notable work in this field, but the problem has not yet arisen for many other scholars dealing with Paul, beyond the recognition of the presence of vice and virtue lists in the New Testament, lists which have their counterparts in the literature of the Stoics and in that of Hellenistic Jews.

Particularly interesting and suggestive in this connection is the monograph, *Die Haustafeln* by Karl Weidinger, for the light that it throws upon the teaching found in these ethical sections which form the conclusion of the several Pauline letters. There is one example of this particular pattern in the writings of Paul, Colossians 3:18 ff. The other New Testament examples are in the later literature. Weidinger's monograph traces this "household" pattern of Christian teaching in pre-Christian teaching. There were two avenues of approach by which the pattern might have entered early Christian teaching, either by way of the Stoic literature or by the Hellenistic-Jewish literature. The fact of such rigidly formulated ethical teaching according to a given scheme makes it appear all the more reasonable that Paul appropriated, from whatever source he found it, ethical teaching that met his needs in ministering to his communities. There is the definite probability that early Christian ethical teaching was absorbed out of pagan moral teaching and was Christianized through the addition of Christian terms. Weidinger likens Paul to the author with his material before him, choosing what he will use and then molding it to suit his purposes and tastes. The present writer has given due weight to these German researches and separates the teaching of the ethical sections from that of the more primary parts of the several Pauline letters. The technical terms used to describe these respective sections are "paraenetic" and "non-paraenetic" which derive from the Greek *par-aineō* (to advise).

The approach to Paul through his social experience in the vital situations in which he was involved shifts the emphasis from the sphere of the intellectualistic to that of the more warmly human. The theologians have dwelt upon his *ideas;* the present study would analyze his *behavior* in the effort to find his practical bases for the achievement of the good life in the varied human relationships of his experience. Paul himself is the major and primary source-material for the study. His letters are very self-revealing. We learn how he handled difficult human problems. It is altogether possible that a careful study of Paul himself, in conflict-situations and out of them, is of much more value in understanding his motivation of human conduct than is any survey of Stoic or Jewish ethical teaching, useful as these undoubtedly are for purposes of background. But the method of collecting literary parallels and the appeal to *ideas* will never yield adequate data on which to base our judgment about the things that touched his life at its center.

CHAPTER I

AN ETHICAL PROBLEM: MUST GENTILES BECOME JEWS TO BE CHRISTIANS?

THE name "Christian" originated in Antioch, an important center of that new religious movement within Judaism which arose in Jerusalem after the crucifixion of Jesus. The distinguishing feature of this new group was the conviction that the crucified Jesus of Nazareth was no other than the long-awaited Messiah. This Palestinian group is usually designated "Jewish-Christian" to distinguish it from those Christian groups outside of Palestine. The propriety of this usage has been questioned recently.[1] It is generally recognized that the transition to Gentile territory was effected early and that the New Testament is a product of Gentile Christianity. Less general is the recognition that Gentile Christianity preceded Paul, whose letters constitute our most valuable source of information about the movement to which he gave his life. Paul wrote in response to the needs of his Christian communities, as crises arose, with no thought of the uses which his writings would serve in the far future, a future which to Paul was nonexistent. There is no such primary source for pre-Pauline Christianity.

The Jewish population of Jerusalem was not a strictly

[1] Donald W. Riddle, "The So-called Jewish-Christians," *The Anglican Theological Review*, XII (1929), 15-33. A Bibliography for each chapter appears at the end of the book.

homogeneous group. Palestinian Jews spoke Aramaic, but there were sufficient Greek-speaking Jews to necessitate a separate synagogue in the Jewish capital (Acts 6:9). These same divisions were perpetuated in the new society, whose form of community organization increased the difficulty of administration as the numbers increased. In response to the complaints of the widows of Hellenistic Jews that they were being neglected in the daily distribution of food, a committee of seven Greek-speaking Jews, headed by Stephen, assumed the responsibility of that aspect of the common life (Acts 6:1-5). Stephen, it appears, was an eloquent preacher as well as an executive, and from the synagogue of Hellenistic Jews an attack was directed against him which launched the earliest persecution of the new movement in Jerusalem (Acts 6:9-14; 8:1-3). This persecution was not directed against the Twelve. Their leaders remained in Jerusalem, which is a commentary upon the quality of their Judaism. Among the persecuting group was Saul, the Tarsian Jew (Acts 8:1-3; cf. Gal. 1:13, 23), who within a very few years became an ardent advocate of the new faith and sanctioned the practice that later plunged the church into its first controversy, a bitter conflict which hinged upon this issue: must Gentiles first become Jews to be Christians?

§ 1

Paul worked for twenty years as a Christian missionary before he wrote one of the letters that we now prize so highly. Fourteen of those years he sums up in the simple statement that he went to the districts of Syria and Cilicia. These silent years were preceded by a fortnight's visit with Peter in Jerusalem and were followed by an important private conference with the Jerusalem leaders. His work

AN ETHICAL PROBLEM

in Syria and Cilicia was thoroughly independent of the Jerusalem group. He was not acquainted with the Christians of Judea, except by reputation, as the persecutor who had become the advocate of the religion which he had tried to stamp out. As a fanatical young Jew, devoted to his religion, he had been violently opposed to Hellenistic Christianity to the point of willingness to persecute its leaders;[2] to destroy the new faith would be a religious act.

Paul dates his Christian life from his conversion, which he interprets as the direct act of God with the express purpose of commissioning him as apostle to the Gentiles. It was an overpowering experience which sent him to Arabia for a time—how long he does not state—then back to Damascus. He spent three years in Arabia and Damascus —it is probably safe to infer work in and around Damascus with the Hellenistic Christians there. He became involved in some kind of trouble in Damascus, for he tells the Christians in Corinth how he escaped the governor by being let down in a basket from an opening in the wall, while the city gates were being watched (II Cor. 11:32-33). Immediately after this escape he visited Peter in Jerusalem, where he also met James, the Lord's brother (Gal. 1:18-19). This is his first contact with Jerusalem Christianity of the non-Hellenistic kind.

Seventeen almost silent years marked by one thrilling escape and a visit of two weeks with Peter! Paul is not writing his autobiography; therefore the fleeting glimpses of his past that he reveals from time to time are seized upon all the more eagerly because they are so very incidental. Were those silent years thoroughly devoid of the kind of experience that was so common in the decade 50-60

[2] W. Heitmüller, "Zum Problem Paulus und Jesus," *Zeitschrift für die neutestamentliche Wissenschaft*, XIII (1912), 320-37.

as shown in Paul's extant letters? Were there no such tense situations as drew forth his letters? With those letters before us it is difficult to see Paul working quietly and effectively in harmony with his churches with no first-class conflict to lend color to the situation. Had he no personal enemies in Syria and Cilicia as he had in the Galatian communities and in Corinth? Was he never in prison as when he wrote to his loyal friends at Philippi? Of the four communities in which Paul later worked and to whom he wrote, only the Thessalonians and the Philippians receive his whole-hearted commendation.

The Christians in Thessalonica had suffered persecution at the hands of their Gentile neighbors (I Thess. 1:6; 2:14) and were having their own troubles when Paul wrote to them after Timothy had brought him the welcome news that they were standing firm in their faith with true courage (3:6-8). Such persecution was a natural product of the social situation. The Roman Empire was tolerant of many cults, the pagan cults were tolerant of each other, membership was not necessarily limited to one. The exclusiveness of the new cult (cf. I Cor. 10:14-24) and the social limitations which it put upon its members would account for a considerable measure of friction between the Christians and their pagan neighbors and friends. This was the case a generation later when the cult of the Emperor was at its height and the Christians refused to participate in the popular ceremonies. Paul had told the Thessalonians that persecution was probable (I Thess. 3:3-4) and he takes satisfaction in the fact that these Christians were bearing their persecution as the Christians of Judea bore theirs from the Jews (I Thess. 2:14).

The trouble in Philippi seems to have its roots in the

AN ETHICAL PROBLEM

Jews, unless Lohmeyer is correct in his hypothesis that the whole letter reflects a two-fold martyr-situation, that of Paul in Caesarea and that of the Christians in Philippi. It does not seem necessary to posit persecution by the state to account for the Philippian situation. The persecution under Nero was not general, that under Domitian was still a generation away. Paul's most bitter anti-Jewish polemic is Philippians 3:2-9, which may be intensified by the actual circumstances in the city from which he is writing. While Paul admits more imprisonments than any other apostle (II Cor. 11:23) he gives no hint as to their place. The variety of speculation which his omission has precipitated does not serve to inspire confidence in the certainty of knowledge at that point.

The letters of Paul give a few hints on the content of his Christian message in this early period. The first Christian creed may be the two items of Romans 10:9, "For if you confess with your lips that Jesus is Lord and believe in your heart that God raised him from among the dead, you will be saved." Paul tells the Corinthian Christians certain traditional features of the faith which he had received (I Cor. 15:3-11). Of utmost importance in the early preaching was the story of Jesus' death and resurrection, and the vision experiences which had been vouchsafed to certain chosen individuals and groups. What Paul preached to the Thessalonians was very similar to the Jewish proselyte propaganda except for the important addition that the Messiah had come, and would come again. The monotheism and the polemic against idols would carry weight with Jews, although other features would be less welcome (I Thess. 1:9-10). In part, at least, Paul's preaching was in harmony with the message of the Jerusalem group. He made one important departure from the practice of that group. He admitted uncircumcised Gentiles to membership in the new movement. When he went to Jerusalem after the fourteen silent years in Syria and Cilicia, he was accompanied by Barnabas, his fellow-missionary, and by Titus, a fine example of Gentile Christian (Gal. 2:1 ff).

What led Paul, the Tarsian Jew, to such a radical departure from accepted standards of the group with whom he wished to be in harmony? What would have happened if he had not made this particular concession to Gentile prejudices? A partial answer lies in an understanding of the social situation. Jews of the Diaspora were accustomed to see Gentiles in their synagogue meetings. There were many Gentiles to whom Judaism as a religion appealed. It was free from polytheism; it taught and practised a high type of morality; it carried on a missionary propaganda; it welcomed proselytes. Many Gentiles were willing to be connected with the synagogue in this "associate-membership" fashion, but they would flatly refuse to become members of the Jewish race by circumcision, which the proselyte must be prepared to do. Cicero expresses the Roman feeling toward the Jews near the middle of the first century B.C. when he says,

While Jerusalem was flourishing, and while the Jews were in a peaceful state, still the religious ceremonies and observances of that people were very much at variance with the splendor of this empire and the dignity of our name, and the institutions of our ancestors. And they are the more odious to us now, because that nation has shown by arms what were the feelings toward our supremacy. How dear it was to the immortal gods is proved by its having been farmed out to our contractors, by its being reduced to a state of subjection.[3]

[3] Cicero *Pro Flacco* xxviii. Translated by C. D. Yonge, Bohn Classical Library (London, 1867), II, 455.

AN ETHICAL PROBLEM

Philo, Paul's distinguished Alexandrian contemporary, describes his experience as a member of a delegation to the Emperor Caligula, which throws some light upon the Roman regard for the Jews in the first century of the Christian era. The Emperor showed little courtesy and dismissed the embassy with commands to leave Rome. Philo is keenly conscious of enmity to his race, and he implies that nothing but the protection of the government saves the Jews from their fellow-citizens.[4]

The testimony of Cicero and Philo is corroborated by that of the Jewish historian, Josephus, and of the well-known geographer, Strabo. Josephus' interesting work, "Against Apion," is an extended refutation of the charges that pagans were wont to bring against the Jews. Strabo insists that the Jews have degenerated since the time of Moses, whom he regards as a wise man.[5]

Paul knew all this and did not vitiate his missionary activity by demanding the impossible. His Christian life had begun in an overwhelming emotional experience, and experience had taught him that that emotional experience was duplicated in many uncircumcised Gentiles. Normally Jews did not act according to this religious pattern; theirs was a more sober type of reaction. But Gentiles accustomed to the more highly charged atmosphere of the mystery cults needed an emotional experience that would approximate that of their early religious experience, and in ministering to this need Pauline religion took on a new aspect.

[4] Philo, *On the Virtue and Office of Ambassadors*. All citations from Philo are from C. D. Younge's translation, Bohn Classical Library, IV, 177-80.

[5] Strabo xvi. ii. 35-39. Translated by Horace Leonard Jones, Loeb Classical Library (New York, 1917). See E. Schürer, *The Jewish People in the Time of Jesus Christ*, Div. II Vol. II, p. 275, n. 183, for further sources on Gentile attitudes toward Jews.

Paul's picture of his second visit to Jerusalem is a very pleasing one. He told the Jerusalem leaders what he preached. He had Titus with him, a fine example of Gentile Christian, uncircumcised, but bearing the true mark of the Christian, the Spirit. It was agreed that Gentiles would not have to become Jews before they might become Christians. A division of the field was made. Paul and Barnabas were to continue their work with Gentiles, Peter and James to continue theirs with Jews. The missionaries to the Gentiles were to bear in mind the poverty of the Judean Christians.

While Paul insists that he went to Jerusalem in obedience to a "revelation," there is an underlying social situation here which may have caused sufficient sleepless nights to produce a vision experience. There were those, Paul tells the Galatians, "who stole in secretly to spy upon the freedom which was ours in Christ Jesus that they might enslave us again. Nor did we at any time yield in subjection to them, in order that the truth of the gospel might remain yours" (Gal. 2:4-5). This experience antedated the work in Galatia since Paul can point to the issue as he faced it with the leaders of the Jerusalem Christian community. The fact that Paul purposely presented his case to the leaders in private, lest his present or past effort turn out to be futile, shows that he did not desire to be as independent of the Jerusalem leaders as he insists that he was. The Jerusalem community was the mother-community. It had prestige at this early period, and Paul saw clearly that if those zealous for circumcision were to carry the Jerusalem leaders with them it would mean the ruin of years of work and a schism in the Christian group that he was deeply concerned to avert. If circumcision and the Law were to become central and normative for Christians,

AN ETHICAL PROBLEM 17

Paul saw his mission to the Gentiles assume the same character as proselyting for the synagogue. Paul was diplomatic enough to avert this. The pillar apostles pledged their coöperation, and Paul was not required to make membership in the Jewish race a prerequisite for membership in the Christian community.

But winning this one point did not solve the problem, and the earliest controversy within the Christian movement hinged upon this question. There was a "party of the circumcision" headed by James, in spite of his consent to the Gentile mission (Gal. 2:9). After his successful visit to Jerusalem Paul returned to Antioch and worked as before. Here was a church of both Jews and Gentiles, and there was free table-fellowship among Christians regardless of their ancestry. Peter came to Antioch and participated in the fellowship of the common Christian meals until some members of the more conservative Christian group came from Jerusalem, whereupon Peter changed his behavior and would no longer eat with the Gentile Christians. Others followed his example. Even Barnabas was carried away by their hypocrisy. This sudden change of attitude irritated Paul, and he berated Peter in scathing terms before them all: "If you, a Jew, live in Gentile and not in Jewish fashion, how can you compel Gentiles to live as Jews?" (Gal. 2:14.)[6]

This controversy into which Paul found himself plunged is of consequence in any attempt to understand how Paul meets ethical problems—what his sanctions for conduct are, what his type of behavior-reaction is, and how he justifies any given course of conduct. This controversy has produced literally thousands of pages on

[6] Ernest C. Colwell, "Christianity a Gentile Religion in Galatians 2:14," *Anglican Theological Review*, XIV (1932), 42-47.

Paul's idea of justification by faith, that battle-ground of theology, but the underlying elements of the very real social situation which brought forth this famous doctrine are never considered. Why Paul was willing to allow Gentiles to join the new movement without first joining the Jewish race has not been seen as the key to the situation. Rather scholars have spent their energy in explaining Paul's explanations. A social approach shifts the emphasis from his ideas to his behavior.

§2

Must Gentiles first become Jews to be Christians? Paul expresses himself most vigorously on this point to the "churches of Galatia." It is not only unnecessary for Gentiles to join the Jewish race to be eligible for membership in the Christian community, but to do so is setting at naught the central tenet of the new faith, *life in Christ*. This particular letter was forged out of the fires of controversy. Nor does the heat thus engendered leave the single impression of a purifying fire. There are some scars of personal bitterness. Controversy may be necessary but it has its unlovely aspects. What conflict-situation lies behind this "charter of religious freedom?"

There is evidence of bitter factions in the Christian communities: "but if you bite one another and eat one another, look out lest you be destroyed by one another" (Gal. 5:15). In marked contrast to the satisfaction of the Thessalonian and Philippian Christians with Paul, these communities bring certain charges against him. His gospel lacks divine sanction, it is a purely human message that he preaches, he is seeking to please men by appealing to their weaknesses, he is preaching circumcision (1:10-12; 5:11). The charges appear contradictory. This is the very

AN ETHICAL PROBLEM 19

last letter in which one would expect to find Paul charged with preaching circumcision. This fact has led to a fresh treatment of the problems of the Galatian situation and a new solution has been suggested. Professors Ropes and Lütgert see Paul combating two tendencies, the Judaistic and the antinomian. The Judaisers believe that circumcision is necessary for Christians. The antinomians or "radicals" oppose both the Judaisers and Paul. Paul's respect at certain points for the Jewish tradition seems to the latter group entirely unwarranted, while the logic of their position seems abhorrent to him. There is trouble in Galatia, as Paul's "have you suffered so much all to no purpose?" (3:4) implies. He is not explicit, but persecution from pagan or Jewish neighbors would be just as probable here as in Thessalonica, and he makes definite statements about persecution in those communities.

No great time had elapsed between Paul's mission in Galatia and the time of the letter. He is amazed at their sudden change of mind (1:6). The spread of the gospel had been rapid among them. Gentiles responded with avidity to Paul's presentation of the Christian message (cf. II Thess. 3:1; I Thess. 1:9-10). The Galatians had received him with enthusiasm (Gal. 4:12-15), but, like enthusiasts, they were capable of being swerved from one position to another (4:21), and, although they had been "running well," they are now being persuaded to be circumcised (5:1-3, 7). This Paul is most eager to avert. There are no stronger statements in any Pauline letter than in the letter to the Galatians. To Paul there is only one side of the question. He freely and vigorously pronounces his anathema upon the preachers of any other gospel even though they bear heavenly credentials (1:6-9). Their intentions are not honorable (4:17). They are acting from unworthy motives. They fear persecution on account of being Christians. Whether this persecution is from the Jews or the state is not clear (6:12; cf. 4:29). Paul declares them insincere in that they do not observe the Law except in this one respect (6:13). He threatens them, ending with the savage wish for their emasculation (5:10, 12).

The identity of these exponents of circumcision is not wholly clear. It has usually been assumed that they were Jewish Christians from Jerusalem, and that here is the inception of the conflict which met Paul at every turn and hindered his work over a long period of years. Professor Ropes sees no necessity for these assumptions. Local synagogue Jews had succeeded in persuading certain Gentile Christians to accept Jewish rites including circumcision, and these in turn were influencing the whole church. Nor does he accept the idea of a long-continued controversy, but believes that Paul's prompt action was effective and that the Galatian episode ended the propaganda of the Judaisers.

Romans and Galatians have always been considered in close conjunction, but the more recent work of Professors Lütgert and Ropes has opened the whole question anew. They have shown that the letter to the Galatians contains a situation not only analogous to that of Romans, but also to that found in the Corinthian letters. Professor Ropes sees Gal. 1:13—2:14 as directed against the radicals, and Paul's long scriptural argument in chapters 3 and 4 as partially intended for the radicals who are not alert to the importance of the Jewish tradition for Christians. This view accounts for the personal charges against Paul in more satisfactory fashion than the older view which sub-

AN ETHICAL PROBLEM

sumed everything in the letter under the question of the Judaistic controversy.

One thing is very clear. It is no matter of doctrinaire theory with Paul. He feels the situation keenly. He is bitterly disappointed with the Galatians. They had received him with such enthusiasm when they might have despised him on account of his repellent physical condition. He is in such anxiety about them that the only figure adequate to express his anguish is that of the throes of childbirth.

While it is necessary to see this controversy over circumcision in its larger setting and to realize what it would mean in the Pauline communities to have the new movement turn Judaistic, with the certain result of closing the doors against Gentiles, of continuing bitter factions in the present Christian groups, it is no less necessary to see that it is much more than a matter of policy and expediency with Paul that makes him insist that circumcision and Law observance are unnecessary for Gentile Christians. He has discovered in his own personal experience and in his missionary activity that there is another approach to the religious life than by way of the works of the Law. To the Jew the Law was essential. It was the revealed will of God. Man's salvation depended upon his obedience to it. But Paul, Jew though he was, was aware of something more important, quite apart from the Law. In countless Christian meetings he had experienced that new surge of feeling which swept through the group, that strange power which produced such tangible results in their very midst.

§3

Paul grew to manhood in a religious system that did not separate religion and ethics. The two are so closely

THE ETHICS OF PAUL

interwoven in Paul's writings that separation is virtually impossible. An understanding of Paul's religious experience is necessary to an understanding of his ethical teaching and his motivation of that teaching. The religion of Paul is no simple phenomenon, since diverse elements entered into the making of that experience. There is, for example, his life-long devotion to Judaism until the direction of his life was changed by a revolutionary experience which resulted in a transfer of loyalty and a resulting change in conduct. His contacts with other Christians helped shape his own religious experience. Although he did not have the experience of life in the Jerusalem group with its community of goods, his letters show numerous traces of ideas shared with the earlier group. In the intellectual content of his preaching there is a considerable amount of Jewish thought in Paul. But the more vital avenue of approach is through his behavior, and his consequent reflections on that behavior. Here are to be found some startling departures from Judaism, even the Judaism of the earliest followers of Jesus with its difference of emphasis with reference to the Messiah, that center of Jewish hope.

There is rather marked contrast between the religion of Paul as it is pictured in Galatians and in Thessalonians. The letters to the Christians at Thessalonica reveal the traditional content of Paul's preaching more clearly than do his other letters. In part, at least, it is the same message that was being preached while he was still a persecutor of the Christian group, for the belief in the appearance of Jesus in Messianic splendor and power *(Parousia)* was very early. Messianism was a marked feature of this preaching (I Thess. 1:3, 10; 2:19; 3:13; 5:23) involving the resurrection of Christians who had died before the

AN ETHICAL PROBLEM 23

appearance of Jesus, and the suddenness with which the appearance of the Lord would take place (I Thess. 5:1-5). Superficially at least, the Thessalonian letters seem to reveal a message leaning heavily on Jewish thought and imagery; resurrection (cf. also I Cor. 15), *Parousia*, and Day of the Lord. The details of the Lord's appearance are described in the imagery of Jewish Apocalyptic, a literary phenomenon present in Judaism from 200 B.C. to 100 A.D. Paul adapts this imagery to Christian use in II Thess. 2:1-12. The bearing of this upon the origin of the ethical teaching of Paul is direct. Paul uses this kind of material, in common with others, in his missionary preaching. The material had gained a kind of fixity through years of repetition. Paul has no objection to the use of traditional ideas.

The letter to the Galatians, however, is marked by an absence of the traditional. Here there are no emphases on eschatology and resurrection, no primitive confession of faith (as in Rom. 10:9), but a different mode of presentation allied with that of I Cor. 2:1-5. Paul is not conscious that his Christian message is not true Judaism (Gal. 6:16). It is not difficult to understand why the Galatians, living in the region that knew the Cybele-Attis cult, should respond with enthusiasm to this appeal, nor why the Corinthians also familiar with the cult-imagery of the mysteries could be appealed to in this fashion when other methods might fail. Paul reminds the Corinthians that when he came to them he had been discouraged and fearful and that he had determined upon a particular method of presentation of the message of Christ. He decided to cast aside all philosophy and rhetoric and to know nothing but Jesus Christ and him crucified. This was a wise decision, for it brought results that were highly satisfactory to Paul and to the Corinthians (I Cor. 2:1-5). He used this same method with the Galatians as we know from his "who has bewitched you, before whose very eyes Jesus Christ crucified was placarded?" (Gal. 3:1).

Paul discounted the philosophical or rather the intellectual approach, choosing instead the way of emotional appeal, which was the method of the mysteries, and which helped to account for their popularity among the rank and file of men. The story of the crucifixion could compete in worthy fashion with the pantomimes which depicted the sufferings and triumph of any one of the popular deities in the Roman world. It is not easy to imagine Paul speaking as a philosopher. He is much too emotional in temperament, too dogmatic, and far too practical a propagandist to attempt to reach by way of the intellect the classes to whom he appealed. That Paul has been pictured as the theologian par excellence is, in the judgment of the present writer, a gross injustice to Paul as well as to the theologians. His method, by his own confession, was to picture Christ crucified, which moved the emotions. In the tense, highly wrought state that followed, "miracles" were not surprising. It is a thoroughly *spiritistic* religion that we find in Paul.[7]

Spirit is a term that has been much misused. Christian writers have taken satisfaction in assuming the superiority of the Christian religion on the ground of its being a reli-

[7] Even in the letters to the Thessalonians with their greater degree of traditional content there is this spiritistic emphasis too. The church is "in God the Father and the Lord Jesus Christ." The Christian message had come to them "in power" (*dunameis*, I Thess. 1:5). Their joy in trouble was inspired by the "Holy Spirit" (I Thess. 1:6). The message "energizes in you who believe" (I Thess. 2:13). God gives his spirit (*pneuma* I Thess. 4:8); Christians are "in Christ," their salvation comes "through Christ" (I. Thess. 5:9). The admonition not to stifle the Spirit, but to test its utterances points to the kind of religion for which the most abundant data are found in the Corinthian letters (I Thess. 5:16-22). Paul's dualism is evident (I Thess. 1:9; cf. II Thess. 3:3).

AN ETHICAL PROBLEM

gion of the spirit and not of the minutiae of Law observance, but seldom has the real meaning of Spirit been apparent. It is one thing to read into Spirit a modern connotation of true inwardness in religion and assume that Paul supports that idea; it is quite another to realize what this concept meant in Paul's environment and what it meant to him. When Christians understand the full implications of these spiritistic emphases in Paul's writings they will be more tolerant of the contemporary religions, Judaism and Stoicism, in both of which, and in a very real sense, man had to work out his own salvation. Especially in Judaism was he given very detailed directions about what to do. The Law was expounded in the Sabbath meetings of the synagogue and was taught in the synagogue schools. Stoicism was weak in emotional appeal. In fact the ideal of the rigid control of the emotions made Stoicism too austere for the average man, while the social limitations under which Judaism labored kept it more exclusive than the popular cults.

The key to Paul's religion as pictured in Galatians is in 2:16b and 2:20-21—"no one is pronounced acquitted by doing what the Law commands,"[8] and "I have been crucified with Christ. I no longer live, but Christ lives in me. The life I now live in the body I live by faith in the son of God who loved me and gave himself for me. I will not set aside the favor of God. For if acquittal could come through the Law, then Christ died in vain."

This type of religious emphasis comes out clearly in every one of the letters of Paul. What has come to be

[8] For a discussion of Paul's figures of speech see Adolf Deissmann, *Paul: A Study in Social and Religious History* (New York, 1926), pp. 168 ff. which treats among others that of "justification by faith." See also E. D. Burton, *New Testament Word Studies* (H. R. Willoughby, ed., University of Chicago Press, 1927), p. 17 ff. and Richard Reitzenstein, *Die Hellenistischen Mysterien-religionen* (Leipzig, 1927), p. 259.

called the Pauline mysticism is the major feature of Pauline religion. He made use of Jewish Apocalyptic in his Christian message—the near end of the Age was an ever-present expectation, not only with Paul but with his predecessors—but the idea of "Christ in me, I in Christ" is a new note and a non-Jewish one. He has the *pneuma* in him, and he became by its presence in him something that he had not been before. *Pneuma* is a concept not foreign to Judaism. It is an Old Testament idea which comes out clearly in the prophetic literature. The prophets felt the power of Yahweh in them. Ezekiel expressed the idea when he said, "The hand of Yahweh is upon me" (8:1). The Spirit in the Old Testament came and went; it was not a permanent possession as Paul describes it to be. A similar idea is conveyed by the way the possession of the Spirit is described in Acts 2:1 ff., which definitely links up with the Old Testament figure. Scholars have differed about the use of the term in Paul,[9] as to whether it is most closely allied with the Old Testament or with the mystery-cult usage. The latest researches seem to substantiate the latter idea. Possession of the *pneuma* makes the possessor a "new creation" (Gal. 6:15; II Cor. 5:17); what has been added is a divine addition which changes his nature. Paul calls some of the Galatians "spiritual" *(hoi pneumatikoi)* which according to Professor Reitzenstein's definition of the term means a person who has *gnosis* (knowl-

[9] E. D. Burton, *Spirit, Soul and Flesh* (Chicago, 1918), traces the usage of *pneuma*, *psuche*, and *sarks* from Homer through the New Testament usage. He believes the marked development in the usage of *pneuma* with reference to the Spirit of God and the spirit of man is due largely to Paul himself.—P. 188.

Reitzenstein thinks Paul independent of the Septuagint (*op. cit.*, p. 312), and notes that the different meanings of *pneuma* in Paul can be found in the magical papyri, and that Paul therefore is simply using the language of his time. His use of *pneuma* and of *nous* in I Cor. 2:11 and 2:15-16 is similar to the oriental-hellenistic usage (*op. cit.*, p. 184).

AN ETHICAL PROBLEM

edge) added to *pneuma*. The most abundant data on the spiritism of Pauline religion are found in the Corinthian letters. It is present, however, in every letter.

It is very clear in the letter to the Philippians. The evidence of Paul's spiritistic outlook is on every page. Modern translation often obscures this fact which is so plain in the Greek vocabulary. Paul blends the mystical and the eschatological in his confidence about the future, convinced that he who began the good work in the Philippian Christians will complete it for the Day of Jesus Christ (Phil. 1:6). He expects his own fortunes to turn out to his welfare with their help and with the help of the Spirit of God (1:19-20). The beautiful sentence, so often used homiletically "For me to live is Christ . . ." is fundamentally spiritistic.

"For it is God who "energizes" you, both to will and to work . . ." (2:13) is in the same category with Paul's confident assertion "I can do all things through him who makes me strong," where the verb is *endunamoō*, a dynamic term (4:13). Paul also uses the technical *en kuriō* or *en Christō* (4:10). He urges the Christians to stand firm *en kuriō* and promises the peace of God as the consequence of their being *en Christō* (4:1, 7; cf. 4:19). Paul prides himself only *en Christō Iēsou* (3:3).

The central passage for this point of view is the one that follows his repudiation of his ancestral faith, where he alludes to all his formerly prized advantages as "refuse" (*skubalon*). Phil. 3:8-11 is one of the best statements of the Pauline mysticism that we find in Paul, and its position, following the list of advantages of Judaism, makes its use all the more effective. Paul is convinced that all those advantages must be set aside in order to enter fully upon the new status.

Indeed I consider all things as loss when compared with the surpassing worth of the knowledge of Christ Jesus, my Lord. For whose sake I have lost everything, and count everything refuse, to the end that I may gain Christ and be found in him, not having my righteousness that of the Law, but that which comes through faith in Christ, which is the very righteousness of God and is grounded in faith. I would know him, both in the power of his resurrection and the fellowship of his sufferings even to a similar death, if by that I might attain to the resurrection from among the dead.

This is plain mystery-cult terminology, very significant in the light of those popular religions. Paul goes on to say that he has not yet attained full initiation, is not yet made perfect, and he uses the technical term of the mysteries, "completed initiation" *(teleios)*.

The Galatian letter contains a thoroughgoing repudiation of the Law as a means of securing God's acquittal on the Judgment Day (2:16). Paul admits that those who seek acquittal through Christ alone still sin—this is contrary to his theory but it is an ever-present fact of experience—but he insists that this is not equivalent to saying that Christ encourages sin (2:17). What he feels to be wrong is the return to Law observance in the face of the Christian's new status "in Christ." Peter's vacillating position had called forth his wrath in this connection. Some of Paul's most radical statements are ". . . if you submit to circumcision, Christ does you no good" (5:2). "You who seek acquittal by means of the Law are cut loose from Christ, you have fallen away from God's favor" (5:4). ". . . for in Christ Jesus neither circumcision nor uncircumcision counts for anything . . ." (5:6). "There can be no Jew nor Greek, there can be no slave nor freeman, there can be no male nor female, for you

AN ETHICAL PROBLEM

are all one in Christ Jesus" (3:28). This is thoroughly Pauline and just as thoroughly un-Jewish.

Paul regards the Law as a form of slavery (5:1). Until the coming of Christ the whole of the human race had been enslaved by the "elements of the world" *(stoicheia tou kosmou)*, probably best understood as great cosmic evil powers which held the world including man in their control. This idea was widespread even among the intelligent. Astrological ideas exercised a mighty grip upon the minds of men, since these ideas were as integral a part of the thought-world of the ancients as the concept of natural law is a major feature in the world-view of the modern man. In Paul's mind the power of the "elements" *(stoicheia)* had been broken when Christ prevailed against them (cf. Col. 2:15). The Galatians had been slaves of this kind, and now to go over to the Law with its observance of days, months, seasons, years would be just as irrational as to want to go back under the control of the *stoicheia* from whom they had been so powerfully freed (Gal. 4:8-11).

Paul launches into a long argument from Scripture to prove his point. The Christians of Paul's day were not like the Marcionites of a century later, who wanted to cut the Christians loose from the Old Testament. Rather, ancient Scriptures were an asset to the new religion. The presence in the communities of Christian teachers presupposes instruction in the Scriptures (as the Christians interpreted them) as well as other things essential for new converts (Gal. 6:6; cf. I Thess. 5:12). Difficult as it seems for such an appeal to be intelligible to Gentile Christians not long removed from paganism, Paul made it, on the assumption that his readers would get the point of the argument.

Those who are inclined to rate Judaistic practices for Christians too highly are reminded that Abraham received the promise of God four hundred and thirty years before the Law arose (3:17). In fact, the Scriptures pronounce a curse upon all those who rely upon Law (3:10). The Law was a later addition designed to last only until Christ. "For if a Law, which could have given life, had been given, then acquittal would have come through that Law. But the Scriptures show all mankind as under sin, so that the promise grounded in faith in Christ might be given to those who have that faith" (3:21-22). Up to the time of Christ the Law functioned in the same way as a slave ministers to a young child. Such an arrangement may be necessary for a time, but it is certainly temporary.

Using the figure of inheritance, Paul passes to the statement that the heir, as long as he is a minor, is in no better position than a slave. By this analogy Paul shows that this was the status of mankind until Christ, but after Christ men were no longer slaves to the Law, but sons of adoption, made so by being ransomed. The common figures of adoption and of sacral manumission drive the point home to the readers. Paul also makes effective use of their willingness for Law by using one of the few allegories which he ever employs. He shows from Scripture the superiority of the new religion over the old by his treatment of the story of Hagar and Sarah and their children: Jerusalem, typifying Jews or Judaisers, in slavery with her children; Sarah, the heavenly Jerusalem, free, promised many children. Just as Hagar's child persecuted Sarah's, so the Jew persecutes the Christians. There is nothing left but to drive out the child of the slave-girl,

AN ETHICAL PROBLEM 31

the practical equivalent of which is to get rid of the Judaisers (4:1-5; 21-31).

§ 4

As shown above, there is an intimate relation between religion and ethics in Paul as there was also in Judaism. In the Graeco-Roman world, however, ethics was the concern of the philosopher not of the religionist. Paul carried into Christianity Judaism's interest in the combination of ethics and religion. Since the function of the Law was to produce a people fit for God's judgment by virtue of obedience to His commands, religion and ethics could not be separated. The Law prescribed what to do. It was man's business to do it. By doing what the Law commanded man achieved an ethical character as well as performed a religious act. Paul's repudiation of the Law forces him to a different motivation of conduct. He takes the only logical step he can take. If man is helpless, unable to work out his own salvation, yet if by the free gift of God appropriated through faith he secures acquittal in God's judgment, it follows that the ethical results, while present, have a different source. They are no longer naturally acquired, but now have a supernatural sanction.

As in all the letters of Paul except those to the Christians in Corinth there is in Galatians the section of ethical teaching, here found in 5:13-6:10. It seems clear that there was basis in Paul's social and religious experience for such teaching as this, that it was not purely theoretical, designed to meet arguments about what a non-legal religion might expect, but that by hard experience he knew that these fledgling Christians—in Christ though they were—did succumb to the desires of the flesh. The current of antinomianism which Professors Lütgert and

Ropes find in this Galatian situation seems quite in order in a region that knew the Cybele-Attis cult. Judging from Paul's comments on conduct befitting the Christian which are found in every letter it seems certain that Paul had to combat the common pagan attitude which ranked the sex appetite in the same class as the appetite for food and drink. He attempts to set marriage upon a higher plane than that practised by the Christians at Thessalonica. Adultery, he warns them, is avenged by God, who insists upon a pure life sexually, and the Christian who disregards this fundamentally important matter is disregarding not man, but God (I Thess. 4:3-8). The fact that the lists of virtues and vices which he uses in Galatians have their counterparts in other literature shows that the popular Stoic preachers had this condition to contend with too and that the synagogue railed against it as well. Paul is not peculiarly Jewish in his outlook here.

The content of Paul's ethical teaching is not new. Just as it is evident that Paul's preaching is not created *de novo* for each occasion, it is equally evident that his moral teaching was not formulated to meet each individual situation. This comes out clearly in the sections of each letter devoted to ethical instruction. As stated above, the technical term for this type of material is "paraenesis," and these sections are called "paraenetic" sections. The major paraenetic sections in Paul's letters are: Rom. 12-15; Phil. 1:27-2:18; 3:17-4:1; 4:4-8; Col. 3:18-4:6; I Thess. 4-5. The Thessalonian section shows the fact of previous formulation clearly. Here the general nature of early Christian teaching appears. Paul refers to the instructions he had given them, on the authority of the Lord Jesus (in response to "revelation"?). They are to live as he had

AN ETHICAL PROBLEM

lived, "to please God." This is religious motivation of the ethical life. It is not a new principle.

There is evident desire for status and reputation in the eyes of the outside world; hence the mention of the desirability of harmony in community life and the belief in economic independence (I Thess. 4:10-12). Paul combats the laziness of certain individuals in this group who had adopted an anti-social attitude in view of the near end of the age (I Thess. 5:14; cf. II Thess. 3:6-12). This situation would hardly be peculiar to the particular community that Paul is addressing, and the warning against it is in the section of more formal stereotyped teaching. Such a warning may point to the probability that this human weakness was accentuated by the prevalent belief that the end of the world, which would obviate any necessity for thrift and industry, was near. In connection with the details about the appearance of the Lord *(Parousia)* there is the admonition to alertness, calmness, in short, to conduct that befits those sharing so great a hope (I Thess. 5:5-10).

The latter part of the paraenetic section in Thessalonians is similar in tone to Romans, 12. The demands upon the Christians are high; the kindness which is appropriate to one who is "in Christ" leaves no room for petty human revenge. There is to be no spirit of retaliation. There is plain recognition of human frailty; there are the idlers, the despondent, the weak, toward whom the Christian is under obligation. This is all so very general, so clearly not peculiar to any one situation that it seems necessary to infer that here we have current Christian teaching, which throughout the years of missionary effort had been found good, and which it was necessary to give again and again, for the words of II Thess. 3:2, "for not everybody has faith," were repeatedly proved true.

The injunction to tender dealing with the sinful is characteristic of this early Christian ethic (Gal. 6:1). The tendency to temptation even among the "spiritual" is also characteristic, and the admonition against self-conceit is one of the most common warnings addressed to early Christians. Paul's was an individualistic religion; men were to stand on their own feet, bear their own loads, yet help in a spirit of love to bear the loads of the weak (Gal. 6:2, 5). There is, however, the sense of Christian community life as well as individualism in Paul's "As we have opportunity, therefore, let us do good to all, especially to those in the household of the faith" (6:10). The emphasis is similar when he urges the Philippians not to act from selfish motive or from vanity, but to be willing to bring the interests of others abreast of their own (Phil. 2:4-5).

Paul urges the Philippian Christians to be like lights in the darkness of the world (2:15). This is a high standard to attain. It means no grumbling, no disputing; rather are they to prove that they are blameless children of God in the midst of a crooked and wayward generation (2:14-15). He cites the pride which he will feel when he can present them as the fruits of his labor on the Day of Jesus Christ. He sets up himself as their ethical norm, along with those Christians whose lives approximate his. There are those who live unethically, whose lives cause Paul grief, who are enemies of Christ (3:17-18). They are not "new creations in Christ Jesus," but are of the earth earthy. The Christians, on the other hand, are potential citizens of heaven, whose bodies Christ will trans-

AN ETHICAL PROBLEM 35

form at his coming (3:20-21). Paul explains the whole idea of the resurrection body in I Corinthians, 15.

Philippians 4:4-8 is quite stereotyped. There is the plea for forbearance, the mention of the *Parousia*, the admonition against anxiety, the exhortation to prayer with thanksgiving. These attitudes and actions, added to their being "in Christ" will bring to them the very peace of God. This beautiful virtue list of 4:8 is similar in tone to the popular moral philosophy. Paul closes the section with an added appeal to them to follow the example of life which he had set them (4:9).

The sphere of Paul's originality is clearly not to be sought in his ethical outlook; but in his teaching on the motivation of conduct he strikes a new note. It is the Spirit that produces love, joy, peace, patience, kindness, goodness, faithfulness, gentleness, and self-control. The Stoics who stressed the virtues expressed in such lists had no such supernatural aid. Man achieved these qualities of character by his own strength. Not so with Paul, who clearly bases his ethics upon the possession of the Spirit. There is ethical dualism in Paul when he sets the flesh *(sarks)* in such sharp contrast with the spirit *(pneuma)*. The common vices belong to the natural man. They can be overcome only by the addition of the supernatural essence, the Spirit. Man must become what he was not, a "new creation in Christ Jesus." It is this assumption that brings Paul into difficulties with certain Christians who are convinced that they have this new addition, but who do not connect its function with the control of the natural human appetites. Paul's originality lies in his conception of the individual Christian as under the guidance of the Spirit, and in his conception of the community as formed of Spirit-guided individuals. This outlook is what is peculiar to him.

It is thus clearly impossible to separate religion and ethics in Paul. For example, in I Thess. 5:23 there is this blending of images, "May your spirit, soul and body be kept complete and without fault at the coming of our Lord Jesus Christ." Here are the spiritistic and the ethical intimately bound up with the apocalyptic outlook. An even better illustration is found in Phil. 2:1 ff. This passage expresses the relationship between Pauline religion and ethics admirably. "So if there is any appeal in Christ, if there is any persuasion of love, if there is any fellowship of the Spirit, if there is any affection and sympathy, make my happiness complete by living in concord, with the same love, the same attitudes, the same mind." Again, "I pray that your love may increase more and more in discernment and insight to the end that you may test what is excellent in order that you may be sincere and blameless as you wait for the Day of Christ, filled with the fruit of righteousness which comes through Christ to the glory and praise of God" (Phil. 1:9-11). Here the religious and the ethical are pictured as ministering to an apocalyptic consummation. The ethic is religiously motivated. Righteous character comes from Christ; its purpose is to minister to the glory of God.

Paul uses the idea of the humility of the preëxistent Lord as an incentive to humility in a human situation where it is needed (Phil. 2:6-11). This is basing an ethical appeal religiously, which is a common form of ethical motivation in Paul, found in the less formal ethical teaching as well as in the special sections devoted to ethical precepts. The fact that it is altogether legitimate to make the distinction between paraenetic and non-paraenetic data

AN ETHICAL PROBLEM

should not obscure the probability that Paul had a share in the formulation of this type of Christian teaching *(paraenesis)*, for his conversion was early in the period of Christianity's rise and his interest in problems of conduct was constant. It is very probable, however, that the mind of Paul is more clearly revealed in the vital, living parts of his letters than in the sections which he approved but did not entirely formulate.

In the letter to the Galatians Paul's treatment of the problem of the necessity of circumcision for Gentiles is marked by a great deal of defense or rationalization. It is with the rationalization that many writers on Paul expend most of their energy. If we start from Paul's *behavior* instead of from his *ideas*, a different light is at once thrown upon the matter. Paul points out the purity of his Judaism in the past (1:13-14) and further insists that the Christians who are "in Christ" are the true Israel of God (6:16). No amount of intellectual defense makes of Paul a good Jew from the point of view of behavior. He did not live as a good Jew was expected to live—one may cite his practice at Antioch as a single example—he admitted uncircumcised Gentiles into the Christian family of the faith. When he strikes a snag and the question of his free practices comes up, accompanied by strife and friction in his communities, he begins to rationalize to provide a defense for his practice. But the fact remains that the practice came first; then the defense of it. The letter to the Galatians is an attempt to appeal to them by argument.

There is reason to believe that the root of Paul's difficulty is to be sought in his temperament. Paul's emotional nature is clearly revealed in every letter. Here we find that intolerance which is willing to anathematize an enemy, that sense of self-sufficiency in apostolic credentials, that tense emotion which keeps him on the heights or in the depths most of the time. It is not difficult to understand Paul's preference for the emotional approach to the religious life, to see why it was so satisfying for him to feel himself a "new creation" and to share the exhilarating accompaniments of the Spirit in the Christian meetings. Yet there is clear evidence that Paul's nature rebelled at the logical conclusion of his theory of freedom from the Law; and when Christians sought to justify licentious behavior from Paul's central emphasis in his Christian teaching, he is forced to the defense of his ideals.

Many of the most vivid pictures of Paul show him in the midst of conflict. In such cases Paul does not calmly reëxamine his position but he defends himself and his practices against attack and rationalizes his side of the controversy. The Judaisers had logic on their side. They could point to the example of Jesus and his disciples. Paul defends himself against his Judaising opponents by appeal to Scripture, no doubt sincerely believing that he has the true interpretation. When some Christians carry his doctrine of freedom to its logical conclusion, he makes an intellectual defense. Where personal enmity develops, he answers in kind and with the utmost self-assurance. There is one side to the issue and it is invariably Paul's side.

CHAPTER II

THE PERSONAL EQUATION IN CORINTH: A CONFLICT OF IDEALS

PAUL'S letters to the Christians in Corinth are the best available source of information on a wide variety of subjects of interest to the student of early Christianity. Nowhere is there more illuminating evidence on the character of the religion preached and practised by Paul. Nowhere is there as complete data on the character of Paul himself. In a number of important respects these letters are most revealing.

Here we are permitted to see how a Pauline church functioned. This is valued information which, it may be safely affirmed, leaves most modern Christians disposed to be charitable toward the defects of their own Sunday morning services. Not many would wish to imitate the service of the Corinthian church. Here is found that precious bit of tradition about the Lord's Supper which has become a part of the ritual of many modern groups, coupled with the mutually exclusive sacramentarian view of the cult-meal of the Christians which is an important aspect of Paul's outlook. Here too is Paul's most detailed description of the resurrection body, his delineation of the events that are to inaugurate the New Age, and the earliest account of the vision-experiences of the followers of Jesus after the death of their leader.

Here is the dubious comfort that church quarrels are no modern phenomenon, that even the leaders were not in perfect harmony. Perhaps the simplicity of the apostolic church is not to be coveted after all. A group of Corinthian Christians were much dissatisfied with their apostle. They found many kinds of fault in him, from his personal appearance to his lack of real apostolic credentials. He is equally sure that many of them are not at all what they ought to be, and in the operation of this indubitable clash of personalities we receive much valuable information on the Corinthian Christians and on Paul.

The Corinthians have some major problems on their hands,[1] which Paul tries to help them meet. Sometimes he is misunderstood (I Cor. 5:9-11); sometimes he is disregarded (II Cor. 10-13); sometimes he wins a great victory (II Cor. 1-7). All these facts are available in the Corinthian letters without the necessity of a final judgment on such details as their chronology or indeed on any point of criticism on which the energy of scholars has been expended.

§ 1

In any effort to reconstruct, on the basis of Paul's testimony, the social situation in the Christian community at Corinth, the people of that community are of first importance. In I Cor. 1:4-9 Paul is either using a formal courteous approach or he is speaking of the Corinthian Christian's potentialities when he says, ". . . there is no gift that you lack even while you are eagerly expecting the coming of the Lord Jesus Christ, and at the Day of our Lord Jesus Christ he will establish you unreprovable" (1:7-8). This type of approach is the customary one with Paul; he is usually appreciative and tactful, at first.

[1] These problems are discussed in Chapter III.

THE PERSONAL EQUATION IN CORINTH 41

The polite address over, he plunges at once into the major issue, the presence of factions in the Christian community at Corinth. "Chloe's people" have brought him information about the quarrels that are rending the community life (I Cor. 1:11). He is in Ephesus at the time (I Cor. 16:8-9), plans to visit them later (16:5-6), commends Timothy to them, asking that they treat him well. Four parties are mentioned, which, presumably, have adherents in the community; those of Paul, Apollos, Cephas, Christ. Apollos declines to visit Corinth, even though Paul urges him to do so (I Cor. 16:12). Apparently he is not leading the faction that has attached itself to him. It seems useless to add to the speculation about the personnel of the "party of Christ." Exactly opposite points of view have been reached by scholars, some of whom think that they were extreme Judaists, others that they were antinomians, still others that there was no fourth party, but only three.[2]

While we may never be sure about certain details, there are conclusions that can be drawn on the basis of the evidence that Paul offers. We get glimpses that reveal the social status of at least part of the Christian group when Paul quite frankly points out that "in the eyes of men not many of you were wise, not many were powerful, not many were well-born" (I Cor. 1:26). In fact, Paul is certain that the world would consider them ignorant, weak, low, and insignificant (I Cor. 1:27). Their social status is revealed, too, in their willingness to rush into court with any trouble they may have with one another instead of trying other methods. This constantly getting into trouble reflects discredit upon them; it is not done by

[2] Hans Lietzmann, *An Die Korinther* I. II (dritte Auflage, Tübingen, 1931), pp. 6-7, summarizes the details of scholarly opinion on the question of the parties in Corinth.

the best people. Apparently they steal from each other (I Cor. 6:8), and Paul's explicit statement "Some of you were once such people," following this catalogue of error, human weakness, and sin: "immoral, idolaters, adulterers, effeminate, given to unnatural vice, thieves and greedy, drunkards, railers, robbers," depicts a group in which the lower elements of society in Corinth were present, if not predominant. Clearly such leaders as Stephanus, Fortunatus, and Achaicus, mentioned in I Cor. 16:17, for whom Paul urges appreciation and coöperation, must have had a difficult task on their hands.

Another interesting sidelight on the social situation in Corinth is found in what Paul reveals about the practices at the Lord's Supper. When the congregation meets, it divides into cliques, which Paul deplores, but somewhat ironically states may be necessary or inevitable. He pictures each hurrying to his own supper; the poor person who had no food with him goes hungry, while his Christian neighbor gets drunk (I Cor. 11:20 ff.)! The moral situation in Corinth, to borrow Paul's phrase, is "nothing to boast about." A flagrant case of immorality is going unpunished, and the attitude of the group is even worse than the offense itself, for there are those who "are puffed up with pride over it" (I Cor. 5:2).

Of course it would not be fair to assume that the majority of Christians in Corinth were the dregs of Corinthian society, but it is fair to conclude that most of them were not of high social status. In all probability they were average people belonging to the working classes, neither better nor worse than the citizens of other cities. They get into the New Testament headlines, to use a modern illustration, because certain conflicts arise which concern Paul very intimately, about which he writes to them with no thought that he is unwittingly furnishing source-material for the attempted reconstruction of early Christian history.

We must recognize a certain bias, too, in our materials. There is clear evidence of personal hostility to Paul in II Corinthians, chapters 10-13. But the situation of hostility, or at least of dissatisfaction, was present at the time of writing I Corinthians. There are those in the group who feel superior to the rank and file of Christians in Corinth (I Cor. 3:18); Paul has two quotations of Scripture ready for them (I Cor. 3:19-20). All is not in harmony when Paul can remark, "It means very little to me that I am judged by you or by any human tribunal. I do not even examine myself" (I Cor. 4:3). There is a good deal of boasting by Christians, and Paul sets out to puncture this unwarranted conceit upon the part of some (I Cor. 4:7-8, 10), who have been "puffed up with pride" as if he did not intend to visit them (I Cor. 4:18).

I Corinthians, chapter 9 offers evidence that throws light upon the dissatisfaction of part of the Christian community with Paul. There are those that want to investigate him (9:3). His apostleship seems to be doubted (9:2), and his answer turns on the question of support of apostles—some are being supported—(9:12) and the Corinthians seem unable to understand Paul's refusal of that privilege. Paul preaches because he cannot help preaching, and his reward is the opportunity to offer a free gospel (9:17-18).

There are indications in I Corinthians that point to a tendency toward antinomianism upon the part of certain Christians. Paul has a good deal to say about *gnosis*. To use the ordinary translation "knowledge" is misleading, for this is a term that does not denote the result of an intellectual process but is rather allied with mystery-cult terminology. What the word means to us was not in the Christian use of it. Reitzenstein points out that the term "mysteries of God" and "knowledge of God" belong together, and that Paul, in the use of such terms, agrees with the usage of Hellenistic mysticism.[3]

There is a group in Corinth who believe themselves to have this *gnosis*. Paul attempts to deflate their unwarranted egotism: "*Gnosis* makes people proud, love is what builds character. If a man thinks that he has some *knowledge* he does not yet know it as well as he needs to know it (8:1-2). In the famous thirteenth chapter Paul contrasts "knowledge" with the supreme Christian virtue, love; ". . . love is not envious, it does not boast, it is not puffed up with pride. It does not behave dishonorably, it is not self-seeking, it is not roused to anger, it does not think evil nor rejoice in wickedness. . ." (I Cor. 13:4-5). This is a reflection of a real attitude motivated by a real situation.

They are in danger of thinking themselves beyond good and evil. Paul answers, "So he who thinks he is standing, let him look out lest he fall" (I Cor. 10:12), and "All things are permissible, but not all things are for our advantage, all things are permissible, but not everything builds character" (I Cor. 10:23). The attitude toward the flagrant case of immorality in their group points to the fact that antinomianism was present.

While the element of personal hostility is present in the first letter, it overshadows everything else in Chapters 10-13 of the second letter. The charges that Paul's opponents make against him plainly reveal that the Corinthian clash is partly due to his qualities of temperament and of personality. We see those charges by way of Paul's

[3] *Die Hellenistischen Mysterien-religionen* (Leipzig, 1927), pp. 295, 300.

pen and must recognize the probability of colored reporting. Paul is telling the story. He is two-faced, they say, cowardly when with them, bold when away (II Cor. 10:1). He acts from worldly motives and boasts altogether too much of his own authority (II Cor. 10:2, 8).

They found fault with his personal appearance and with his preaching; neither was up to the standard of his letters (II Cor. 10:10). If the tradition preserved in Acts 18:24 is accurate, there is basis for the preference upon the part of some for Apollos. "He was an eloquent man, able in his use of the Scriptures . . . and he spoke with fervent zeal. . . ." There is evidence, however, that Apollos did not lead his faction but rather that he was loyal to Paul. There were other leaders in the Christian community at Corinth of whom Paul's opponents approved. "For when someone else comes and preaches another Jesus from the one I preached, or you receive a different spirit from the one we received, or a different gospel from the one you accepted you bear with it beautifully" (II Cor. 11:4). Paul calls these men "apostles," admits his lack of skill in address, but insists that he is not lacking in *gnosis*, which they prize so highly (II Cor. 11:5-6). They have not been able to understand his working without pay (II Cor. 11:7), something which their leaders, whom Paul sees as false apostles (II Cor. 11:13), apparently did not do. "For you bear with it if a man makes you his slaves, or devours your substance, or takes you in, or is inflated with pride, or slaps you in the face" (II Cor. 11:20). They had insinuated that Paul was clever, and while he did not take pay himself, he tricked them through sending others (II Cor. 12:17), which charge Paul indignantly repudiates. That this personal hostility belongs in the group in which the antinomian tendencies were found is indicated in Paul's misgivings about the conditions that he may find in Corinth when he visits them. His own words are clear:

I am afraid that perhaps there may be wrangling, jealousy, hot anger, self-seeking, slander, gossip, conceit and confusion, and that when I come back, my God may humiliate me before you, and I shall mourn over many who have kept on sinning and have never repented of the impurity, immorality and sensuality in which they have lived (II Cor. 12:20-21).

Yet they seem to have been sure that they belonged to Christ (II Cor. 10:7).

Various chronologies have been adopted for the Corinthian correspondence. In general there is agreement that II Corinthians is composite, but opinion is divided as to the details of its component parts. Many of these details do not affect our problem, such as whether the chapters about the collection are one letter or two, whether II Cor. 6:14—7:1 is a part of the letter mentioned in I Cor. 5:9, a bit of early Christian paraenesis, or an integral part of II Corinthians. A more interesting problem is whether II Corinthians, chapters 1-9 (with or without 6:14—7:1) follows or precedes the letter of reproof in II Corinthians, chapters 10-13. It is one thing to see in II Corinthians, chapters 1-7 an answer to the situation aroused by chapters 10-13 which then would be considered highly successful in its outcome. It is another to see, with Lietzmann, in chapters 10-13 the necessity of nothing more than a sleepless night in order to have them follow naturally upon the two most tactful chapters in Paul.

Paul mentions a letter in II Cor. 2:4 ff. and again in 7:8 ff., and there have been attempts to find that letter in Paul's extant correspondence. There is evidence of a situation in Corinth, in which serious trouble had died

THE PERSONAL EQUATION IN CORINTH 47

down and a troublesome individual had been disciplined by the group. There are difficulties in the way of seeing that letter as either I Corinthians or II Corinthians, chapters 10-13. Neither fits the case. The notorious offender of I Corinthians, chapter 5 might be such an individual, but that incident is such a small part of the total situation depicted in I Corinthians that it seems unsafe to adopt such a hypothesis, while II Corinthians, chapters 10-13 presupposes a group or faction hardly to be reduced to one individual by a letter of reproof. Of course there is no necessity for insisting that some part of Paul's extant correspondence is that particular letter. The letter that caused Paul so many tears may quite well be lost. A candid reading of II Corinthians, chapters 10-13 does not reveal tears as dominant in the situation.

If we see in II Corinthians, chapters 10-13 a letter of reproof highly successful in its results, we must also admit that the effects were not lasting. I Clement reveals a situation in Corinth, which seems to point to the fact that the conditions revealed in these extant letters of Paul continued, or at least blazed out a generation or so later. Clement alludes to the presence of rash and self-willed persons in the Corinthian group.

... the abominable and unholy sedition, alien and foreign to the elect of God, which a few rash and self-willed persons have made to blaze up with such a frenzy that your name, venerable and famous, and worthy as it is of all men's love has been slandered (I:1).

Clement is extravagant in his praise of the Corinthian Christians for their honorable past (I:1; II:4) and launches into a long array of Scriptural examples of worthy conduct. The present trouble is over the title of bishop (XLIV:1). Clement urges against schism

48   THE ETHICS OF PAUL

(XLIV) and alludes to the early parties mentioned by
Paul (XLVII:4-5) in these words:

But that partisanship entailed less guilt upon you; for you were
partisans of Apostles of high reputation and of a man approved by
them. But now consider who they are who have perverted you,
and have lessened the respect due to your famous love for the
brethren.

There is no way of knowing the situation in Corinth between the letters of Paul and the letter of Clement near the end of the century.

Although it may not be possible to reconstruct the situation in Corinth with any feeling of certainty in detail, these letters nevertheless constitute a major part of our most important source-material for an understanding of Paul's religion, of his method of meeting ethical problems, and of his personality.

§ 2

A careful study of the way Paul meets a situation of personal hostility to him, even charges of a preponderantly unjust nature, reveals clearly that at least part of the difficulty which Paul met in Corinth and elsewhere was due to a trait in his personality, which made him a difficult person with whom to work. *Self-assurance* is one of the major characteristics of Paul. It is next to impossible to imagine Paul thinking of himself as in the wrong in a given situation. He was always abundantly and pre-eminently right. He was right when he set out for Damascus determined to stamp out the young movement which was so assuredly wrong. He was right when he later saw in Christianity true Judaism. Such psychology is likely to stir up conflicts upon any provocation.

This extreme self-assurance is grounded in his religious experience, in his conviction that he has seen the Lord, that he has been specially commissioned by God for his task (I Cor. 9:1-2; 15:8; 9:12; II Cor. 2:17; 5:20). Paul's sense of authority was very fully developed. It is fairly easy to see how his opponents might feel that he boasted too much about it (II Cor. 10:8). One feels that at times he overworks the idea of apostolic authority; in fact there is no place at which Paul is less open to admiration from a purely human point of view than in this very matter. The fact that he justifies his authority by appeal to his divine commission does not make this aspect more pleasing in the give and take of ordinary human relationships. The authority is from the Lord; to build up, not to tear down (II Cor. 10:8). Perhaps it is not from a man's enemies that we get a fair judgment; yet surely a hostile situation throws some light that would not be available otherwise, and it should not be ignored, nor dismissed as worthless in the attempt to get an objective picture of the man. Paul threatens a "bold attitude" for his next visit, if things continue as they are (II Cor. 10:2, 11). Paul's sentence in 10:18 shows where he stands, "For it is not the man who commends himself who is really commended; *it is the man whom the Lord commends.*"

The apostolic prerogative is a limited one. Certain false teachers are claiming it in Corinth and apparently are making good their claims (II Cor. 11:12-15; 12:11). Paul will not grant to these workers whom the Corinthians approve the same status as his. Rather they are sham apostles, dishonest workmen, pretending to be apostles of Christ (II Cor. 11:13). Their doom will fit their actions, for their behavior is certainly not such as to commend them (II Cor. 11:15, 18). Paul appeals to experience as well as to revelation to substantiate his claims to apostolic authority. He calls the Corinthians the "certificate" of his apostleship (I Cor. 9:2). The signs of an apostle were present when he was with them: "signs, wonders, marvels." II Cor. 12:11-13 is illuminating. The Corinthians forced him to boast *when they ought to have been voicing their approval.* Paul expects to spare nobody on his third visit. He will *prove* his apostolic right, will prove convincingly that Christ speaks through him (II Cor. 13:3). He is prepared to punish, and to carry through what he says in his letters (II Cor. 10:6, 11).

It is not only in the chapters where he is on the defensive that he is fully conscious of his apostolic dignity. He sent Timothy to them because "he will remind you of my ways of doing things, methods which I teach everywhere in every church" (I Cor. 4:17); and "What do you wish? Am I to come to you with a club or in a spirit of love and gentleness" (I Cor. 4:21)? Apparently he has no desire to upset the *status quo* (I Cor. 7:17, 24). "These are my orders in all the churches." Paul distinguishes between his own commands and those of the Lord, which are by revelation (I Cor. 7:10). When he has no command of the Lord, he substitutes his own opinion as that "of one who by the mercy of the Lord is trustworthy" (I Cor. 7:25). When he assumes that widows would be happier as widows, he adds "I think I have God's spirit" (I Cor. 7:40).

He defends his action in not taking pay (I Cor. 9:17-19; cf. I Thess. 2:6, 9), but stands firmly on the right to be supported, to marry, to live as the other apostles live (I Cor. 9:12). "Though I am free from all control, I have made myself a slave to all, so as to win the more"

THE PERSONAL EQUATION IN CORINTH 51

(I Cor. 9:19). Paul acknowledges himself an opportunist. He becomes all things to all men, "and I do it all for the sake of the gospel, so that I may share in the good news" (I Cor. 9:23). In asking the Corinthians not to be hindrances to Jews or Greeks, he adds, "just as I try to please everyone in all that I do, not aiming at my own advantage, but at the advantage of all, that they may be saved" (I Cor. 10:33). Paul valued both the capacity for hard work (Phil. 2:19-22) and harmonious living and coöperation (Phil. 4:2). This attitude, however, did not greatly affect his relationship with those who opposed him. Once within the Christian group of a Pauline church, he felt his authority over them; this comes to light when he speaks of the details of Christian meetings which are to be settled when he arrives (I Cor. 11:34). He orders women to keep quiet in church (I Cor. 14:34), also to wear veils, since he recognizes no other practice in worship, and neither do the churches (I Cor. 11:16). His sense of authority is very clearly revealed in II Cor. 2:9, "For that is why I wrote you—to know how you would stand the test and if you would be obedient in everything." Paul gladly accepted gifts from the church at Philippi and implies that the Philippians earn merit through what they have done for him (Phil. 4:17-19).

In welcome contrast with too much apostolic dignity is his tact when he defines the meaning of the leaders in the sects at Corinth. "What is Apollos? Or what is Paul? Just ministers through whom you had faith as the Lord gave it to each of us" (I Cor. 3:5-6). And in I Cor. 4:1, "The right way for a man to think of us is as Christ's servants and as administrators of the secret truths of God." Of course such servants must be dependable. Even here the certainty of prerogative creeps in; he is set apart to make known the secret truths of God. In spite of his calm, tempered statement as to what he and Apollos really are and his thoroughly fine treatment of the sects, he soon breaks forth into sarcasm. "For who set you apart? What do you have that has not been given you? But if it has been given to you why do you boast as if that were not the case? Are you satisfied already?" When he lays down the law about women keeping silent in church he adds, "Did the message of God start from you Corinthians? Or has it reached only you" (I Cor. 14:36)?

One would expect to find biting irony and sarcasm in II Corinthians, chapters 10-13. A few examples will illustrate. "I do not venture to put myself among those who approve of themselves. They are not showing good sense when they measure themselves by one another, and make comparisons among themselves" (II Cor. 10:12). "You gladly bear with fools, since you are so wise yourselves" (II Cor. 11:19). After a scornful thrust at their self-appointed leaders' treatment of them, he adds, "To my shame I say that I was too weak for that" (II Cor. 11:21). And "For what is there in which the other churches excelled you, except that I did not allow myself to be a burden to you. Forgive me that wrong" (II Cor. 12:13).

Paul can pass from sarcasm and stinging reproof to expressions of deep affection (II Cor. 11:11; 13:11-13; cf. I Cor. 4:14). Paul would justify sarcasm on the grounds of necessity as in 4:14, "I do not write this to shame you, but to admonish you as beloved children." He is an intensely emotional person. He feels keenly in every situation, whether is be one of joy or of distress. He is on the heights or in the depths most of the time. His first appearance among the Corinthians was "in weakness, and fear and trembling" (I Cor. 2:3). He approves of their

THE PERSONAL EQUATION IN CORINTH 53

greeting Titus "in reverence and trembling" (II Cor. 7:15).

The quality of emotion is very different in II Corinthians, chapters 1-7 from that of II Corinthians, chapters 10-13. The former reflects a situation where the church has stood by him, where a situation of anxiety has ended, and great relief surges up. Titus has brought Paul the welcome news. Paul pours out his heart to them. His own words bring out this quality of his personality.

For I want you to know, brothers, about the distress that I experienced in Asia, for I was exceedingly weighed down beyond my power of endurance, until I despaired even of life. I was convinced that the answer was death ... (II Cor. 1:8-9).

For out of much distress and anguish of heart I wrote you through many tears, yet it was not to cause you grief, but that you might know the exceeding great love which I feel for you (II Cor. 2:4).

For if I was beside myself, it was as unto God, and if I am sane again, it is for your sakes (II Cor. 5:13).

I have told you all, men of Corinth, my heart is open to you. Not I but your own affections are cramping you. To repay me, my children, open your hearts to me (II Cor. 6:11-13).

Make room for me. . . . You are in my heart whether I live or die. . . . For all my trouble I am overwhelmed with joy (II Cor. 7:2-4).

For when I reached Macedonia, I could get no relaxation whatever—everywhere there was trouble—fighting without and fears within (II Cor. 7:5).

... he [i.e. Titus] told me of your longing for me, of your sorrow, of your enthusiasm for me, which made me still happier (II Cor. 7:7).

The emotional temperament of Paul comes out clearly, also, in his relations with the Christians at Thessalonica.

He has no enemies in this church; the Christians are behaving satisfactorily, standing firm "in the Lord" (I Thess. 3:8; cf. 4:9-10), which means in conscious connection with the Spirit, usually expressed by the technical *en kuriō* or *en Christō*. This news was such a relief to the harassed man that he pours himself out in terms that seem extravagant to the unemotional western mind, but which would not seem so to the oriental. We have the picture of Paul at prayer, rejoicing over these Christians (I Thess. 1:2), longing night and day to see them (3:10), praying that they may love each other as he loves them, which will insure a condition pleasing to God at the appearance of the Lord (3:13). He describes his affection for them in terms of intimate family love, that of mother and father for their children (I Thess. 2:7, 11). When away from them he longs eagerly to be with them, looking forward to his pride in them at the *Parousia* (I Thess. 2:19). He had been fearful lest they be led astray—into what, he does not say—probably back into their former ways, since the trouble they were having was from their neighbors, and Paul knew the force of social pressure. Their community life seems to be above par from a religious point of view, if we may trust the exegesis of a paraenetic datum (I Thess. 5:11). Paul is very appreciative of the Thessalonians; in fact this letter shows Paul at his best emotionally, even if the emotion does seem a bit too intense. A similar appreciation appears in his letter to the Philippian Christians, another group for whom Paul has nothing but praise (Phil. 2:18; 4:15). He is particularly solicitous for their representative, Epaphroditus, who became ill, and at the time Paul was writing was homesick and distressed (2:25-30).

Paul's reflections on his conduct while at Thessalonica

THE PERSONAL EQUATION IN CORINTH 55

show us the extremely high standards set by him. It was no cheap and easy ethic that Paul lived. He is strong in his conviction that his conduct had been irreproachable (I Thess. 2:10). "You know the kind of life we lived among you for your good" (I Thess. 1:5) might be taken as the text of the description of Paul's ethical attitudes. He points out that the Christian message had been without fraud, wrong motives, or delusion (I Thess. 2:3). There had been no flattery, no greed. He had waived apostolic right to support, and had worked night and day to earn his own living (I Thess. 2:5, 9). He had constantly urged them to make their lives worthy of God (cf. Phil. 2:14-15), which is religious motivation of ethics (I Thess. 2:12). All this taken with what he implies in his irreproachable relations with them signifies that the Pauline ethic, so far as we find it in the situation in Thessalonica, was of a high type. This holding himself up as an example, with the apparent self-congratulation, may possibly indicate a situation in the Christian communities similar to that described in the Didache, where not all Christian missionaries are to be trusted (Didache, xi-xii). It should be noted that this belongs to a later period in Christian history.

Accompanying self-assurance and an intensely emotional temperament, there is also tact. The chapters dealing with the collection (II Cor. 8-9) reveal the possibilities that Paul did not utilize, possibilities at least which do not show very strongly in some of the major situations in which we find him. When Paul exhibits such skill as he does here, it is really amazing to find him attempting to win his ends by other means than by persuasion. For he is a master hand at that art. These chapters might well be used as a manual of instruction in raising money for worthy causes. Why did not Paul stand firmly upon his apostolic prerogative and demand that a certain sum be raised by a certain time? Perhaps there is lacking a note of sincerity in the way he handles the matter—Wrede dislikes these chapters and thinks that they leave a bad impression when read candidly.[4] But to the modern person, accustomed to extravagant advertising and high-powered salesmanship, these chapters come with a refreshing sense of a man's skill in a very human and never easy situation.

He appeals to the sense of rivalry between Greece and Macedonia, tells how the latter overreached his expectations, in fact *begged* to share in the support of their fellow-Christians. Then he turns to Corinth, strikes while the iron is hot, appealing to their *pride* and other good qualities. Of course they will not lack generosity. He does not command; he merely tells them how he feels about it! Since they were the first to propose the collection, as long ago as the previous year, there is no need to say more. He recommends proportionate giving, according to a man's means. Moreover there is not to be the least chance to criticize the handling of this important matter. He points out that the committee will soon be there; "so prove before all the churches the fact of your love and of my pride in you" (II Cor. 8:24).

Paul may have had confidence in the Corinthian Christians, but he took no chances on slipping up on details. Even though it is unnecessary to write to them because of their willingness to help—Macedonia has heard of their enthusiasm, that they have been ready for a whole year—it is well to remind them again, in case some Macedonians come with him, for that humiliation would be too much. Of course the plain fact of the case is that Paul has been

---

[4] William Wrede, *Paul* (Tübingen, 1904), p. 35.

THE PERSONAL EQUATION IN CORINTH 57

playing off the different churches against each other, and he has to make good his boasts on both sides.

Another of Paul's most outstanding characteristics is his capacity for hardships. Paul glories in hardship. This is an abnormal attitude, but it seems normal to him. Using the figure of an athlete he says, "So that is the way I run, not uncertainly. I fight thus, not beating the air. But I beat and bruise my body and make it my slave, in order that after I have acted as the herald for others, I may not be rejected myself" (I Cor. 9:26-27). The famous catalogue of Paul's boasting (II Cor. 11:22-33) shows that he spared himself no hardship whatever. This fact comes out at lesser length in II Cor. 6:4-5 ". . . as a servant of God I commend myself in every way, by great endurance, in troubles, in difficulties, in distress, in wounds, in imprisonments, in tumults, in labors, in wakeful nights, in hunger. . . ." Unquestionably the capacity for suffering for a cause which was vital to him must be ranked as one of the outstanding traits of Paul's character. No one can point to insincerity here. When a man goes through what he endured for the sake of his faith it is evidence of no weak and flabby religion, but rather proof that his religion was of supreme concern to him, the central thing in his life. The fact to remember is that Paul's religion was a functional thing; it nerved him to superhuman tasks.

There is in it something of that quality which comes to light in the pronounced ascetic, who glories in flagellation; there is something of the martyr-complex, which makes the devotee unable to feel the pain in the ecstasy of martyrdom. This quality is fairly clear in the letter to the Philippians. Perhaps the imprisonment experience through which he was passing at the time of writing to the Christians at Philippi colored his emotional outlook. Whatever the reason, the martyr element is clearer in this letter than in the Corinthian situation. He looks upon death as a decided advantage, since it means being with Christ (1:23). He reminds the Philippians that they have been given the privilege of suffering for Christ's sake and urges them not to give up the struggle (1:29-30). He is ready and glad for martyrdom (2:17-18) and pleads with the Philippian Christians to value men like Epaphroditus very highly, for he came near to death for the Lord's sake (2:30). While he feels that death would be an advantage, he expects to see them again and expects a favorable conclusion of his present trying circumstances. Paul is never half-hearted or sophisticated in his religious expression.

To have lived through all the hardships in which he glories would convince him of the help and power of God, and it is this conviction that made Paul so difficult to work with—people sure of God's favor often are—that makes him seem so conceited. Not that his definite boasting gives that impression as much as do the more incidental references. The boasting is saved by the context: "I speak as a fool speaks."

There is much in Paul that grates, even while we recognize his strong points and his probable contribution to emerging Christianity, but when we forget his canonical status, as it were, and see him as a man among men, we realize how much apologetic has been written about him throughout the years by his biographers. Not that the pictures have been untrue; rather they have been half-truths. No one could overemphasize what Paul was willing and glad to endure out of loyalty to Christ. No one would willingly minimize that side of Paul's personality.

And yet, there is the other side of the picture in Paul's own writings. Self-assurance is a primary quality in any well developed personality, but we do not like to see it overdone. Paul did not either, and called it boastful conceit when an opponent indulged in it. Sarcasm may be a justifiable mode of expression; most people wince under it. A strong sense of authority may make for efficiency. Not many people know how to use power over other human beings without overstepping. Paul certainly did not, and his inability to see himself in any way but in the right seems to have made for hostility in more than one situation. It was Paul's major weakness.

§ 3

The religion of Paul is a complex phenomenon. Its most deeply personal aspects show most clearly in the letter which he wrote to the Corinthians after Titus had reported their changed attitude on some crucial matter (II Cor. 1-7). Paul interprets his trouble as intended for discipline, to teach him to rely on God and not on himself (II Cor. 1:9-10). He has found that God is a God of comfort, always ready to cheer the discouraged (II Cor. 1:3, 7:7). In what may be interpreted as an oath, Paul appeals to the reliability of God (II Cor. 1:18). A similar note is found in his interpretation of his physical affliction, which he assumes is from God to keep him properly humble (II Cor. 12:9).

Paul's deepest conviction was the central fact of the indwelling Spirit. "For I am not a peddler of God's message, as many are, but in all sincerity, and from God and before his face, in Christ I speak" (II Cor. 2:17), and "My ability is from God who has made me his minister, a minister of a new agreement which is not in writing, but of the Spirit" (II Cor. 3:6). "It is God who guarantees us and you to Christ; he has anointed us and set his seal upon us and has put his Spirit in our hearts as earnest-money" (II Cor. 1:22).

II Cor. 5:17 is of fundamental importance in Paul's religious outlook, "So if any one is in Christ, he is a new creation, the old state of things has passed away, there is a new state of things." Because this spiritistic emphasis is central with Paul, he can be so sure that the Law is superseded in Christ. There is no conflict with Judaism in these letters as in Galatians; consequently Paul can speak of Judaism more calmly than it is possible for him to do in certain other situations. Judaism is described as Moses' veil, in terms of a familiar Old Testament story, and only union with Christ will remove the veil and reveal the true splendor (II Cor. 3:15). There is no polemic here, simply the statement of the destruction imminent for those who are blind to the truth of Paul's gospel (II Cor. 4:3).

To be "in Christ" is of paramount importance for Paul. He does not say in this correspondence how a person reaches this state, i.e., how the Spirit is acquired. In Gal. 3:1 it is stated that it came through the hearing of the Christian message, not through the keeping of the Law. Acts represents it as coming through the laying on of hands. It is probable that the important rite of baptism had something to do with it, since this was the rite by which the believer entered into union with the Lord of the cult. Since the Spirit was the mark of every true Christian, it may well be that this was part of the sacramental function of that rite.

Paul puts the Cross of Christ central in his message here. His words in I Cor. 2:2 attest this; ". . . For I decided to know nothing among you but Jesus Christ and him crucified." The Cross of Christ marks the passing of Jesus from the earthly to the heavenly sphere; it is in the latter that the Spirit functions. The Spirit comes from Christ and is the real mark of the Christian. Linked up with this is Paul's emphasis on the resurrection. It is basic in his gospel, for that gospel is conditioned at every turn by the power of the risen Lord. The consequences of no resurrection would be the utter ruin of the Christian faith (I Cor. 15:12-19; II Cor. 4:13-14). But the great fact of Christ's resurrection, attested by the presence in their midst of the marks of his power, the Spirit, pledges man's resurrection. If there is no resurrection, why trouble to undergo baptism for the dead which some Christians have done (I Cor. 15:29)? If there were no resurrection, why does Paul fight the beasts at Ephesus, taking hourly risks with his life? If there is no resurrection, ". . . let us eat and drink, for tomorrow we shall die" (I Cor. 15:32).

Paul learned that to make the Cross central was much more effective than to use fine language. His preaching was "in demonstration of the Spirit and of power" (I Cor. 2:4). One of the main elements in his defense of his apostleship was this very thing, "the signs of an apostle were displayed among you with all patience: signs, wonders, works of power" (II Cor. 12:12). The Spirit, to Paul, was more than a figure of speech. It was a powerful reality.

This becoming a new creation is a thoroughly supernatural matter: "all this is from God who reconciled me to himself through Christ and gave to me the ministry of reconciliation, how God was through Christ reconciling the world to himself, not keeping account of men's transgressions, and giving to me the message of reconciliation" (II Cor. 5: 18-19). This language is doubtless colored by the process of reconciliation through which Paul has just been passing with the Corinthian community. It is an evidence of Paul's skill in adapting the central features of his religion to the present situation. It savors of his approach to the Colossians, where he meets those who are attracted by speculation and Gnostic tendencies on their own ground and shows the sufficiency of Christ to meet all needs of Christians (Col. 2:8-15).

Similarly in the Corinthian situation there are those who are tinged with Gnostic thought, who are antinomian in tendency, who set a high valuation upon the supernatural "gifts" of the Spirit, and Paul presents the message of the Cross as a "mystery." Paul represents himself as more "spiritual" than his readers who were but babes "in Christ" (I Cor. 3:1). The real "wisdom" has to be reserved for those who are *teleioi* or initiates. This is mystery-cult terminology. There were three classes of people in Gnosticism: *sarkikoi* (equivalent to *sarkinoi* in I Cor. 3:1), *psuchikoi* (I Cor. 2:14), and *pneumatikoi* (I Cor. 3:1). The mysteries also have three classes: unbelievers, *religiosi* or proselytes, and *teleioi* or fully initiated. The attempt to explain *gnosis* as the first effort at a Christian or religious philosophy, which emphasizes the theoretical elements is a thoroughly mistaken method.[5]

Paul presents the Cross of Christ as the "wisdom of God in a mystery," the message of secret, divine wisdom. It would never be recognized as such by either Jews or Greeks, but it is at this point that God chooses to confound the world (I Cor. 1:25-28). Had the authorities responsible for the crucifixion of Jesus known this wisdom, they would have refrained out of fear (I Cor. 2:8). God reveals to the Christians these unseen things, through his

[5] Reitzenstein, *op. cit.*, pp. 326, 305.

Spirit, which searches out the deep things of God (I Cor. 2:10). Paul and his helpers impart these God-given revelations, in whatever words the Spirit gives to those who can, through the Spirit, receive them (I Cor. 2:13-14). It is this conviction that leads Paul to say, "I have the mind of Christ" (I Cor. 2:16). All this is very esoteric and quite beyond the Corinthians in their present state. They are not to be treated as *pneumatikoi*, but the Corinthians did not all agree with Paul, and the clash already described resulted.

It is through the power of Christ that men become acquitted by God (I Cor. 6:11). The Christian is a temple of God, the home of God's Spirit, a sacred thing (I Cor. 3:17, cf. II Cor. 6:16). The Christian belongs to Christ (I Cor. 3:23). The Christians will judge angels (I Cor. 6:3), presumably at the *Parousia* which inaugurates the future judgment. Paul is confident that he knows the events that are to take place in connection with the appearance of the Lord (I Cor. 15:52-53; cf. I Thess. 4:15-5:3). In a number of passages Paul uses the conception of the Day of the Lord (I Cor. 1:7-8) as a day of testing men's work (I Cor. 3:13), a day on which the Lord will be the judge (I Cor. 4:5). Paul hopes to be able to point with pride to the Christians on that day (II Cor. 1:14). A bit of Paul's Jewish heritage is seen in his idea of the judgment when he says, "For we must all appear before the tribunal of Christ that each may be requited for what he has done while he lived, whether it be good or bad" (II Cor. 5:10). Paul's long exposition of the resurrection body of the Christian came as a result of Gentile difficulty with the whole idea of resurrection which is from Paul's Jewish heritage. He has to adapt a Jewish idea to a Gentile concept of salvation, and it is not an easy thing to do.

The Christians collectively are Christ's body; the individual Christian is a part of that body (I Cor. 6:15). This is one of the fundamental postulates of Pauline mysticism. By virtue of the Spirit of Christ in him, the Christian becomes joined to the Lord of the cult; he is "in Christ." This phenomenon of a group of Christians, all of whom have the same divine increment, constitutes the body of Christ. Paul was realistic here. He conceived the relationship in real fashion. The man who was *en Christō* had something in him which had not been there before. By virtue of it he was a new man.

This spiritistic conception of religion got Paul into difficulties when it began to function in the Christian community. I Corinthians, chapters 12-14 gives a clear picture of this type of religion as it worked itself out in practice and of Paul's qualifications of some of his major premises as they began to tangle the religious and the social situation. It does not require a particularly active imagination to realize that the conception of supernatural presence in the community working without let or hindrance might produce an unenviable situation. And it seems that this was the case. Some Christians while speaking "in the Spirit" had said "Curse Jesus." Paul had to give them a criterion by which to tell when it was a genuine utterance of the Spirit (I Cor. 12:3). There was rivalry among the members of the community over their respective "gifts"—some were rated more highly than others; especially prized was the "gift of tongues" (*glossolalia*).

There is no better place to see the mingling of the Jew and the Gentile in Paul than in this setting. Paul had been brought up in the orderly meetings of the synagogue.

He had come to appreciate this different approach to the religious life, which satisfied the cravings of his emotional nature, and made him feel himself a "new creature." He gloried in ecstasy. But circumstances as they arose in the Christian community showed him clearly that the unbridled use of even anything as good as the "spiritual gifts" *(charismata)* would wreck the community on the side of religious organization, as the idea of being beyond good and evil would wreck an individual or a group from the point of view of morality. So Paul sets out to change the collective mind about the "spiritual gifts."

Paul uses the familiar figure of the human body with its diversity of parts, each part with its peculiar and necessary function, as the best parallel available to illustrate what the Christian community ought to be and how the various "gifts" ought to be used. Every "gift" comes from the same Spirit. God produces them in the different members of the group. These vary but they are all "gifts" *(charismata)*. There should be no more room for jealousy among members differently constituted than there should be for jealousy upon the part of one member of the human body toward another member. There is no unnecessary part of the body, and there is no unnecessary "gift." The Christians, variously endowed as they are, constitute the body of Christ, and they should use their "gifts" for the common good, just as members of the body work together in harmony and perfect adjustment.

Because a situation of jealousy and discord has arisen, because some "gifts" are more valued than others, Paul proceeds to pass judgment upon the relative merits of the "gifts," giving, as he does so, a scale of values. "God has placed people in the church, first as apostles, second as prophets, third as teachers, then mighty works, then gifts of healing, of ministrations, of ruling, of speaking with tongues" (I Cor. 12:28). He urges them to cultivate the higher endowments. The "prophets" rank high in Paul's scale. Reitzenstein observes that Paul connected "to prophesy" and "to speak in *gnosis*" as basic parts of the community cult and used "prophesy" as the mystery communicants did.[6]

Paul then goes on to point out a better way, the way of love, ranking it above the languages of earth or heaven, above the preaching of secret truth and the possession of all *gnosis*, above faith, above property, above even life itself (I Cor. 13). He also points out the futility of the much-prized "speaking with tongues" *(glossolalia)* in public meetings of the church. He values the gift of ecstatic utterance in its place, but that place is assuredly not at public worship (I Cor. 14:8-9). He attempts to institute rules for the conduct of public worship, the central feature of which is, "Let everything be done becomingly and in orderly fashion" (I Cor. 14:40). One needs not wonder that Jews found Pauline religion so unacceptable. One can only marvel that Paul believed Christianity to be good Judaism. Even with Paul's rules for Christian worship there is still much that would strike strangely upon Jewish ears. People come to church with the notion that the Spirit may speak or act through them. Paul would limit the luxury of "speaking in tongues" to two or three people, and only if there is an interpreter present. One wonders what would happen if the interpretation displeased the one who had spoken in the Spirit. In the absence of an interpreter the ecstatic person must talk to himself or to God and not interrupt the service. There are to be no more than two or three inspired messages;

[6] Reitzenstein, *op. cit.*, p. 307.

THE PERSONAL EQUATION IN CORINTH 67

the rest are to listen and ponder. It is quite in order to interrupt a preacher if the Spirit so dictates; real prophets will understand such procedure.

Women are to stifle their urges to speak. Under no condition are they to be anything but silent. This must have come from experience, for it is contrary to Paul's theory as expressed elsewhere, as to lack of sex distinctions of those *en Christō*. Perhaps the women were contentious here as in the matter of veils at public worship.

Paul's religious ideal, it would seem, was a Spirit-controlled community of Spirit-filled individuals. He never gave up this ideal; there is not a letter of Paul that does not show these spiritistic emphases, though we are indebted to the Corinthian correspondence for the really definite information about how such a religion functioned in community life. As already seen, Paul does not state how the spirit is acquired, but from the warning that he gives the Corinthians about avoiding pagan cult meals, lest they take a demon into the same habitation in which Christ dwells, and so lose the good supernatural presence (I Cor. 10:4 ff.), it may be inferred that the Eucharist functioned to keep the presence of Christ in the believer.

This indwelling Spirit is the guarantee of the new body which will be given to the Christian in the future (II Cor. 5:1, 5). Paul is eager to leave his home in the body and make his home with the Lord (II Cor. 5:8; cf. Phil. 1:23). The data in the Corinthian correspondence are so definite as to how the Spirit functioned in a community, and the widely-used term *mysticism* is so vague and so capable of varied interpretation and connotation in the different historical periods that it seems more accurate to designate the Pauline phenomena as *spiritism* in religion.

With this brief survey of the Christians of Corinth,

the personal traits of Paul, and the major emphases of his religious outlook the way is cleared for a better understanding of the man Paul as we shall meet him handling the varied problems as they arise in the Christian community. Some of these are social problems; some are definitely matters of church polity; but with the intimate connection between religion and ethics in Paul, they must be examined in any endeavor to understand Paul's attitude on ethical problems.

CHAPTER III

COMMUNITY PROBLEMS IN CORINTH: NORMS OF CONDUCT

WE must always bear in mind the fragmentary character of our sources of information about the Christian communities founded by Paul. His letters are occasional, designed to meet a specific situation. That he treats one subject at considerable length in one situation and barely mentions it in another is no reason for the hasty conclusion that the problem was nonexistent or unimportant in the other community. In I Corinthians Paul takes up the question of eating meat which had been offered in pagan sacrifices. Are we to infer that this problem was nonexistent in Thessalonica, Philippi, and in the churches of Galatia? To do so would seem to be an unwise procedure. What we are permitted to see in the Corinthian situation is how Paul met that problem in Corinth. In the same letter Paul dwells at length upon the question of marriage. This very common social experience would be equally prominent in the other churches. And was the problem of orderly conduct of Christian meetings, including the observance of the Eucharist, a Corinthian problem alone? One would hesitate to affirm that. Or were the Corinthian Christians the only group who settled their differences in pagan courts?

Broadly speaking, the points of major interest in the

Corinthian situation fall into two classes: those which may be defined as social problems and those relating to church polity. The line of demarcation, however, is not rigid. The two types cross each other at certain points, as in the matter of the observance of the Eucharist and in excommunication from the group of those persons guilty of the more heinous breaches of morality. The matter of eating meat which had been offered in pagan sacrifice was a social problem too; very closely interwoven with the daily life of the people, even though it had religious implications as well. In any situation, whether the religious or the social element is uppermost, the problem becomes an ethical one. We must remind ourselves again that religion and ethics are not to be separated in Paul. The fact of quarrelling and factions in the Corinthian group (I Cor. 1-4) would complicate the adjustment of difficulties in the situations that might arise from time to time.

§ 1

Cumont says, "The laxity of morals at the beginning of our era has been exaggerated, but it was real."[1] It is equally certain that ethical sensitivity was not limited to Judaism although it was keen in that religion. Philosophical speculation had deserted the field of the physical sciences to turn its attention to the problems of morals, and in Stoicism preëminently, as well as in the less influential Epicureanism, the thinking turned to problems of conduct. Stoicism was the philosophical system that held the place of primacy in the Graeco-Roman world of Paul's day. Neo-Platonism which supplanted it was still nearly two centuries in the future. We may not, therefore, as-

[1] Franz Cumont, *The Oriental Religions in Roman Paganism* (Chicago, 1911), p. 42.

COMMUNITY PROBLEMS IN CORINTH 71

sume total moral decadence outside of Judaism and the new Christian movement any more than we may assume a lack of religious interest in the first century of our era.

Corinth was a great commercial city of mixed population, with Roman, Hellenic and oriental strains. The worst elements of Graeco-Roman civilization would be found there. We have already noted the proletarian character of the Christian community at Corinth. It is sometimes inferred from Rom. 1:18-32 and I Thess. 4:1-12, both of which were written in Corinth, that this city represented the extreme of moral degradation. But the fact that Paul makes use of contemporary literary forms taken over from the literature of Stoicism and of Hellenistic Judaism, the material of which clearly exhibits *fixity*, should warn us against the sweeping conclusion that Corinth, of all ancient cities, was the most steeped in vice. We may remind ourselves too of a significant sentence of a generation ago, "It is questionable whether the average morality of civilized ages has largely varied,"[2] before we put Corinth in a class by herself beyond the pale of common decency.

The Christian community at Corinth was struggling with its problems of adjustment, some of which were problems of morality. Paul had written to them (I Cor. 5:9) in such a way as to leave them in doubt about his meaning concerning their relations with immoral people. Paul recognizes the impossibility of hermetically sealing the Christian community from the outside world. Slaves must continue to serve pagan masters. Men must continue in the work they chance to be doing; they have their livelihoods to earn as they did before they became Christians.

[2] Edwin Hatch, *Influence of Greek Ideas upon the Christian Church* (London, 1891), p. 139.

In the major contacts of their lives they are part and parcel of the world around them. Exclusiveness is an impossibility, even if they desired to burn every bridge between them and their past, which is inconceivable. Paul agreed that they could not go out of the world even to avoid immoral people. But what they may not do is to tolerate immoral conduct within the Christian group itself. While Paul affirms that Christians are to judge the world and even angels (I Cor. 6:2-3), presumably at the coming of the Lord *(Parousia)*, he is content to leave to God the judgment of non-Christians at present. The Christians' business is with members of their own group alone.

Paul's ethical standard is rigid: "Do you not know that the wicked will have no share in God's kingdom" (I Cor. 6:9)? Here he is appealing to the motive of reward and punishment. He reminds the Corinthians of the former status of at least a part of them by citing a list of vices in which immorality is prominent, but he goes on at once to remind them of their new status, that of acquittal in the name of the Lord and by the very *pneuma* of God. Moreover, his "Do not be led astray" surely points to the danger of that very thing. There was in the Christian community at Corinth a group who carried the Pauline idea of being "a new creation in Christ Jesus" to unwarrantable lengths and justified licentious conduct on the apparent ground that the spirit was not affected by what the body did. Their idea of *gnosis* differed from Paul's. The background of this is to be found in the Hellenistic dualism of flesh and spirit. The Orphic-Platonic idea of the body as the prison-house of the soul has had far-reaching consequences. This same dualism led in opposite directions, toward antinomianism and toward asceticism. Professor Lake's statement, "I Corinthians shows clearly

COMMUNITY PROBLEMS IN CORINTH 73

that some Hellenic Christians held that having secured immortality they were free to do as they liked with their bodies. Paul insisted on the observance of that morality which was central in Judaism. He had rendered his task difficult by the rejection of the Law . . ." is a good formulation of one of the main problems of Paul. He could conceive of nothing better than excommunication of the wrongdoer from the Christian group, and this he insists upon in the Corinthian situation (I Cor. 5:13).

Paul deals with one case of notorious immorality in the Christian group (I Cor. 5:1-8). Here is the clearest indication in I Corinthians of the antinomian tendency present in that community. Not only are the Christians unrepentant over what was a violation even of pagan law, but they are actually taking satisfaction in it. Excommunication is not their remedy. This Christian is one of the "advanced" ones who pride themselves on their *gnosis*. Even the Gentiles, Paul observes, would not allow a man to have his father's wife. Roman law forbade a man to marry his step-mother even if his father were dead or divorced, and since the verb used *(echein)* indicates a lasting relationship and not a mere incident, the situation was probably one of concubinage. The personal enmity between Paul and this group comes out clearly here (I Cor. 4:19). He is not usually so drastic. In the paraenetic section of his letter to the Galatians he urges the *pneumatikoi* to set the wrongdoer right in a spirit of gentleness (Gal. 6:1). This is much the more common emphasis in Paul, even if he is simply approving already formulated ideals.

But this person who belongs to the group which disagrees with Paul is not to be treated gently. Paul, with them in spirit and having passed judgment as though present, in the name of the Lord has "handed the man over to

Satan for his physical destruction that his spirit may be saved on the Day of the Lord" (I Cor. 5:5). This is not figurative language. Satan was a very real part of the *Geisterwelt* in which Paul lived. Paul distinguishes here between the destruction of the flesh *(sarks)* and the powerlessness of Satan over the *pneuma,* an evidence of his spiritistic outlook. To hand a man over to Satan belongs in the same class of punishment as to anathematize him. Paul could anathematize those who did not agree with him (cf. Gal. 1:8). He expresses a willingness to be cursed if by that means he might insure the salvation of his countrymen (Rom. 9:3).

The use of the curse was common in Judaism and in the Greek world as well, as papyri and ostraka show. Paul was reflecting Jewish practice when he urged excommunication for breaches of morality. The leading men, the elders in Judaism, exercised the power of the ban or outlawry of the guilty individual from the community. Both the ban and the curse have very ancient antecedents in Judaism. Jephthah was outlawed from Gilead (Judg. 11:3 ff.) and Micah restored stolen money because he feared his mother's curse (Judg. 17:1 ff.). Excommunication from the group is only the outward sign of a much more fearful reality in Paul's day. Demons and Satan were real entities to him. The world was in the control of evil supernatural powers (Col. 2:8-15). Only those *en Christō* had no fear. Sending a man out of Christ's group meant sending him out under control of the powers of evil, out of reach of the power of the Spirit. The very real sense of the supernatural to early Christians can hardly be overestimated. The handing a person over to Satan means his bodily destruction, since Satan and his demons cause illness and death. Paul is voting

COMMUNITY PROBLEMS IN CORINTH

for the offender's death when he hands him over to Satan. But because the man has *pneuma* in him, received through baptism at his initiation into the cult, he is fortified against the final victory of Satan. This seems somewhat in line with the claims of the antinomians. Why trouble about ethical standards if the *pneuma* is present? Here is a logical difficulty in Paul's thinking.

The social and religious ostracism urged by Paul in I Cor. 5:12-13 would be effective in proportion to the value placed upon Christian fellowship by the members of the community and the depth of conviction about the superiority of the new religion to those of their own past experience. The curse was a potent power in the early history of religion. The story of Ananias and Sapphira in Acts 5:1-11 conveys the idea of similar power. If, as seems probable, this group mentioned in I Cor. 4:19 and 5:2, 6 is the group against which Paul inveighs in II Corinthians, chapters 10-13, not much social pressure had been exerted by Paul's vigorous pronouncement. Perhaps the personal equation was too strong.

We have an interesting example of righteous indignation vented in Stoic fashion upon a man of good social standing who was detected in adultery. Epictetus does not anathematize:

But if we lay aside this fidelity for which we are formed and make designs against our neighbor's wife, what are we doing? What else but destroying and overthrowing? Whom? The man of fidelity, the man of modesty, the man of sanctity. Is this all? And are we not overthrowing neighborhood and friendship and community, and in what place are we putting ourselves?

Epictetus likens the man to a worthless utensil fit only for the dung-heaps.

Then, will you say, no man cares for me, a man of letters? It is just as if wasps complained because no man cares for them, but all fly from them, and if a man can, he strikes them and knocks them down. You have such a sting that you throw into trouble and pain any man that you wound with it. What would you have us do with you? But I am a man of letters and understand Archedemus. Understand Archedemus then and be an adulterer and faithless and instead of a man be a wolf or an ape; for what is the difference?[3]

Paul's motivation of conduct varies. Upon occasion he appeals to the idea of reward and punishment. In his advice to the community after he so vigorously anathematized the offender, he makes a natural appeal to social experience. He sees the probable effect on the community life of such behavior. He uses a common Jewish figure to illustrate the power of evil conduct over the lives of others. The community is like a mass of dough, the immoral man is like yeast, a little yeast will leaven a large mass. The only safe procedure is to get rid of the yeast; then the life of the community will be pure. I Cor. 15:33-34 strikes a similar note in a different way, "Do not be deceived. Evil associations corrupt good persons. Be soberly righteous and stop sinning, for some of you are ignorant of God. To your shame I speak so."

In Paul's general attack upon the position of the antinomians in 6:12-20 he deserts the natural and social appeal in favor of the spiritistic religious one. Paul is hard set against lax sex-relations, quite probably because of his ancestral religion; yet it must ever be borne in mind that the social experience of many peoples when it reaches expression in the ethical codes of the great religions has this

[3] Epictetus *Discourses* ii. 4. Translated by Elizabeth Carter and edited by W. H. D. Rouse (New York, 1910). All citations of Epictetus are from this translation.

COMMUNITY PROBLEMS IN CORINTH 77

same emphasis. When he attempts to answer those who are claiming full freedom in the matter of sex-relations, apparently putting this form of indulgence on the same plane as the satisfaction of hunger (I Cor. 6:13), he deserts the social appeal and attempts to build up a defense which is utterly devoid of social significance.

"Not everything I may do is good for me," and "I am not going to let anything master me" are quite rational. They might be characteristic utterances of any highminded, ethically sensitive person who valued self-control. A Stoic would be in full agreement. But when he develops his argument against immorality, he shows that the spiritistic element is ever-present. It may be Paul's Jewish heritage that conditions his emotional reactions to the sins of sex, but he certainly does not advance a Jewish argument against them.

"Do you not know that your bodies are part of Christ's body" (I Cor. 6:15)? By virtue of the indwelling *pneuma* the Christian is joined realistically to the body of the Lord. When a Christian has sex-relations with a prostitute, he is bringing the actual body of Christ into this unholy connection. By a bit of ingenious exegesis of "the two shall be one flesh," Paul uses the Scriptures to support his contention that the Christian, by virtue of having this divine substance in him, the Christian who is *en Christō*, is prostituting the body of the Lord with whom he has been joined. It is the Lord who is wronged, drawn into an immoral relationship, because he is in the body of the Christian. This is one of the clearest cases of basing ethics upon religion, as well as being spiritistic in a very bald sense.

In this same argument Paul appeals to the certainty of

the resurrection as a reason against immorality (I Cor. 5:14). The body is the temple of God's Spirit (I Cor. 6:19), the Christian has been bought and paid for, his body is the Lord's (I Cor. 6:20). Paul uses the well-known custom of sacral manumission to illustrate the relationship of the Christian and his Lord. Just as the slave was bought by the deity of the temple, but free in the eyes of men, so the Christian is the slave of Christ, bought and paid for.

It is possible to understand Paul historically, to see the origin of his ideology, to understand the problem which he faced, to appreciate his insistence upon a high type of morality, and yet to see the inadequacy of this type of defense. His argument is based upon the very important tenet of his religious outlook, his spiritistic belief. It is a labored intellectual defense that he makes, conditioned by the circumstances in which he found himself. He is trying to meet the antinomians on their own ground, that of a special relation to Christ and *pneuma*, by virtue of which they felt safe from any conceivable danger.

We may not find fault with Paul for not emphasizing the social implications of unbounded liberty in this area of sex-relationships and the dangers to community life of anti-social conduct. We may not insist upon his being a sociologist, but we may and must analyze his bases of the good life, before we blindly see him a norm for modern individual or social ethics. We may *not* make him conform to any modern theological image unless we are apologists or authoritarians. It is not particularly against Paul that we find his basis of conduct as intellectually indefensible at times as we would find his order of service in a Christian meeting distasteful.

COMMUNITY PROBLEMS IN CORINTH 79

§2

Unquestionably the major social problem which Paul attempts to meet in I Corinthians is that of marriage. This is a problem that touches life most intimately. When the Christian movement found its way into the centers of population and began to win adherents, it was faced with the very practical question of these common social relationships, and none was more common than this one. The Christian community must operate under pagan laws of marriage and divorce, must either adjust to pagan ways of thinking about marriage and sex or break down the pagan customs and behavior of its new converts. I Corinthians, chapter 7 touches upon various angles of this side of social experience. It is instructive to read this chapter and compare it with the more rigidly formulated pattern of Col. 3:18 ff. The Corinthian advice is much more vital and bound to contemporary life. In such a comparison it is easily seen which type of literary expression comes out of the immediate social situation.

Nowhere do the social implications of Paul's eschatological outlook come to view as plainly as in I Cor. 7:26-35. Paul justifies the *status quo* "in view of the present distress" (7:26). "The appointed time has grown very short." "For the present shape of the world is passing away" (7:29, 31). It is common for Christian writers to account for the phases of Paul's attitude toward marriage that are distasteful to them by appeal to this fact: that his advice was conditioned by his expectation of the near end of the age and consequently may be discounted, but that we may still find in Paul the bases of much that we value in our own ethical and religious outlook. This is a natural inference, but it does not follow that his opinion on the various problems connected with marriage is thus conditioned, i.e., problems not necessarily connected with the preservation of the *status quo*. Paul is other-worldly in his outlook. The *Parousia* is near, the Lord will return, Christians will share in the judgment, and all this is to happen during his lifetime, as he confidently asserts in this same letter (I Cor. 15:51; cf. I Thess. 4:13-18).

The religious motivation appears in Paul's judgment that marriage is a "worldly care." Whole-hearted devotion to the Lord is not to be expected of the married. Both man and woman put pleasing the other ahead of the Lord's work. Paul believes that devotion to the service of the Lord redounds to the advantage of the one who renders such service with undivided attention. Yet he disclaims any desire to "put a halter on" them (I Cor. 7:35) and definitely states that it is no sin to marry (7:28) although it is a sure way of having worldly trouble. Preserve the *status quo,* remain as you are; if married stay married; if not, do not marry (I Cor. 7:26-27). This judgment of Paul's arises out of his eschatological belief. Since the time is short, and there are so many outside the pale of the Christian group, it behooves Christians to engage in service for the Lord.

Epictetus advances the same argument against the advisability of the Cynic philosopher's marrying that Paul does when he insists that marriage prevents whole-hearted attention to the things of the Lord. Epictetus says,

But in the present state of things which is like that of the army placed in battle order, is it not fit that the Cynic should without any distraction be employed only on the ministration of God, able to go about among men, not tied down to the common duties of mankind, nor entangled in the ordinary relations of life, which if he neglects, he will not maintain the character of an honorable

COMMUNITY PROBLEMS IN CORINTH

and good man? and if he observes them he will lose the character of the messenger, and spy and herald of God.[4]

Epictetus, however, would apply this only to the philosopher, not to the rank and file of men. For these he says the principal things are:

Engaging in public business, marrying, begetting children, venerating God, taking care of parents, and generally having desires, aversions, pursuits of things and avoidance in the way in which we ought to do these things, and according to our nature.[5]

Paul's attitude on various problems in connection with marriage makes this chapter one of the best in which to study his motivation of conduct. His ethical outlook may be judged from the way he reacts to the problems in the life of his churches on this very common matter of marriage. If Paul sets up any norms, they should be in evidence here.

Asceticism as well as antinomianism was a normal consequence of dualistic thought about flesh and spirit. Some members of the Corinthian community have been wondering if the ascetic ideal is not to be followed even by those who are married. Paul had doubtless congratulated himself upon his single state in their hearing while he was still with them, since it was a point in which he took great satisfaction. He frankly admits that he would like to have them all as he is, blessed with the gift of continence, but he realizes that God has not bestowed that particular gift with a lavish hand. It is rare.

Excellent as it is for a man to remain unmarried, the exigencies of the social situation press in upon Paul, and he realizes that he must compromise with his ideal. Faced with this necessity, he makes the necessary adjustment and

[4] Epictetus *Discourses* iii. 22.   [5] Epictetus *Discourses* iii. 7.

states that it is better for each man to have his own wife and each woman her own husband because there is so much immorality current. Paul does not vitiate his advice here by too much rationalization. Marriage is not a holy state to him; at best it is the lesser of two evils. He seems to rate desire for sex-relations as the only reason worth considering for marriage at all.

There is the problem of the ultra-conscientious, those who are seriously doubting the propriety from the Christian point of view of sex-relations within marriage. Would not continence be the ideal? One might expect Paul to decide for abstention here, but he does not. He fully recognizes the conjugal rights of husband and wife and declares against continence as a policy for the married, except for religious ends, and then only for a brief period and by mutual consent. This is not new with Paul. Jews and Greeks had long considered that sex-relations rendered the participants ritualistically unclean. Here Paul is acquiescing in a position much older than the Christian movement.

For the unmarried, including widows, Paul counsels celibacy. "It is an excellent thing if they can remain single as I am" (I Cor. 7:8). Marriage is to be sought only by the incontinent, for in spite of its difficulties it is better than promiscuity in sex-relations or constant desire for such relations. It is distinctly a compromise measure between the highest and the lowest.

To the married he speaks the Lord's command, not his own. There is to be no divorce upon the part of either partner. If a woman separates from her husband, she is to remain single or be reconciled to him. It is natural to see in this one of Paul's rare appeals to the historical Jesus. At times the context of his commands from the

COMMUNITY PROBLEMS IN CORINTH 83

Lord clearly shows that the commands are spiritistically mediated, but the fact that this is in line with the synoptic tradition of the earliest gospel at least leaves the probability of its being a bit of genuine Christian tradition from the pre-gospel stage of Christian history. This is very un-Jewish advice, as the Jews, except for the school of Shammai, favored rather easy divorce. The section of the church which produced Matthew's gospel agreed with Shammai when they put in the extenuating circumstance of adultery as the sole ground for divorce.

But the marriage problem was not so easily disposed of. Paul was faced with the very common situation of mixed marriages, that is, marriage in which only one partner had become a member of the new cult. Here Paul is forced to compromise. If the people concerned are satisfied with their arrangement and wish to continue living together, Paul would not insist upon disrupting the union. In such a case there must be no divorce for religious reasons only. Paul's course here is conditioned by circumstances. He saw the dangers inherent in such a union, but until the Christians were thoroughly inculcated with the ideal of exclusiveness for the new religion they would go on as before. Gradually, and only gradually, could a new attitude be developed, for the pagan cults were tolerant of each other. We do not know that Paul was successful in all the arguments by which he sought to root out pagan practices. Intolerance has been listed as a factor in the final triumph of Christianity over the pagan cults, but that belongs to a later period.

Once he admits the advisability of non-interference in marriages where only one partner is Christian, he has to rationalize his judgment. Here again his spiritistic belief furnishes the key to the rationalization. The pagan partner is under control of demons, which he takes within himself at cult meals (cf. I Cor. 10:20-22), but the Christian partner has the *pneuma*, that divine addition to his nature that makes him "a new creation in Christ Jesus." Just as the heinousness of prostitution was due to bringing the body of the Lord into connection with that of a prostitute, so it is possible to counteract the presence of the demon in one partner, by the more powerful *pneuma* of the other and the ensuing offspring are not unclean but holy.

This settled to his own satisfaction, Paul's opportunism is even clearer in his willingness for this marriage to be dissolved if the pagan partner wishes to separate (I Cor. 7:15). This judgment is religiously based in "God has called you to live in peace."

Suppose the couple are no longer able to live in peace. We may assume a case where the wife is the Christian member of the marriage, since it is sometimes said that women are more easily led into new religious alliances than are men. Suppose this woman with all the zeal of the new convert has been strongly influenced by Paul and refuses all contacts with her pagan neighbors, refuses to go with her husband to pagan festivals at any one of the many temples in Corinth, becoming in his eyes a kill-joy. Suppose they quarrel over the wife's attending the evening or early morning meetings of the Christian cult, whose meetings were held at night so that the slaves and poor workers might attend. Suppose she agrees with Paul that pagan gods are demons and airs that view in the privacy of the family circle. Suppose she speaks "in a tongue" at the Christian meeting and glories in that fact. Suppose she succumbs to the ideal of continence within marriage as those of I Cor. 7:1-7 did. It is clear that mixed marriages con-

COMMUNITY PROBLEMS IN CORINTH 85

tained very potent possibilities of becoming intolerable.[6] Small wonder that Paul was relieved to appeal to the fact that God wished them to live in peace and that marriage was not *slavery*, but that the unbelieving partner might go away. After all, he remarks, the one reason for staying together, viz., the possibility of converting the unbelieving partner, is very problematical, the Christian cannot know if the pagan partner will be saved or not. The children by virtue of the *pneuma* of one parent are clean, but in the short time remaining before the *Parousia* there can be no certainty of saving the unbelieving partner. One might raise the question whether the great number of Christian *widows* were from such marriages. By the time the Pastorals were written the church was seeking to define just who was to be considered a real widow (I Tim. 5:1-16).

There is no unanimity of opinion on the meaning of "virgin" in I Cor. 7:36-38,[7] but an increasing number of scholars see in this passage the reflection of the beginnings of an institution which reached its full flower in the third century and is revealed in the writings of Tertullian and Cyprian, two great fathers of Latin Christianity.[8] Briefly speaking, a virgin was a woman devoted to the service of the church. She might be living with a Christian man in "spiritual" union. As is clearly shown by Tertullian and Cyprian the continence expected did not always materialize, and it seems to be the case here. Paraphrasing, Paul's attitude is something like this: "Go ahead and marry, it is

[6] Christians were called "haters of mankind" in the early second century.—*Annals of Tacitus* xv. 44. Translated by Church and Brodribb (London, 1895).

[7] In the American translation of the New Testament Professor Goodspeed interprets virgin as "engaged girl."

[8] Tertullian, Part III, *On the Veiling of Virgins* (Ante-Nicene Fathers Library, Buffalo, 1885), IV, 27 ff.

Cyprian, Treatise II, *On the Dress of Virgins* ANF V p. 430 ff. and Epistle LXI *op. cit.*, pp. 357-358.

no *sin*, you are now in the same condition as other folks who find it necessary to marry to avoid immorality." He cannot forbear noting, however, that the man who *can* live in the celibate state with his virgin will be doing the superior thing.

There is no one ethical norm that Paul sets up in the problem of marriage. He has one rule when both are Christians, another when one is Christian and one pagan, and still another when the class of women known as virgins figures in the situation. Paul simply does the best he can in the differing circumstances and justifies his judgment by rationalization. A few things are clear. He considers marriage a prophylactic measure against immorality. Celibacy is the ideal state. Marriage hinders religious service. He does not have the faintest notion, apparently, of any social significance to marriage or of any satisfaction to be gained outside the realm of the physical. His confident expectation of the imminent end of the age would preclude the social emphasis. Why beget children and train them if there is no long look into the future either for the Christian group or for society (I Cor. 7:29-31)?

This keen expectation of the end of the world is also brought out in what he has to say to slaves. "Let each remain in the calling in which he is called. Were you called a slave? Do not let it trouble you. But even if you can become a free man, rather make the most of your present opportunity" (I Cor. 7:20-21). This argument is religiously based, for the slave *en Christō* is a freedman of the Lord, and the free man *en Christō* is the Lord's slave. Nothing matters but the becoming a "new creation in Christ Jesus," and this does not depend upon social status.

COMMUNITY PROBLEMS IN CORINTH 87

The Stoic attitude is expressed by Epictetus in his words to a master whose slave had displeased him:

Slave yourself, will you not bear with your own brother who has Zeus for his pro-genitor, and is from the same seeds and of the same descent from above? But if you have been put in any such higher place will you immediately make yourself a tyrant? Will you not remember who you are and whom you rule? that they are kinsmen, that they are brethren by nature, and that they are the offspring of Zeus?[9]

Here too, a religious motivation of conduct is offered. With Epictetus, the slave, as well as the master, is a son of God, by virtue of his constitution as a man. All men are brothers. With Paul, the slave as well as the master comes into a peculiar relationship to God, by virtue of sharing the same *pneuma*.

Seneca, Paul's contemporary, is eloquent on the essential kinship of man. He writes,

I am glad to hear that you live on friendly terms with your slaves. This befits a sensible and well-educated man like yourself. "They are slaves," people declare. "Nay rather they are men." "Slaves!" "No, comrades." "Slaves!" "No, they are unpretentious friends." "Slaves." "No they are our fellow-slaves, if one reflects that fortune has equal rights over slaves and freemen alike." . . . They are not enemies when we acquire them; we make them enemies. . . . Despise if you dare those to whose estate you may at any time descend even when you are despising them. . . . Each man acquires his character for himself, but accident assigns his duties. . . . Show me a man who is not a slave; one is a slave to lust, another to greed, another to ambition, and all men are slaves to fear. . . . No servitude is more disgraceful than that which is self-imposed.[10]

---
[9] Epictetus *Discourses* i. 13.
[10] Seneca *Epistle* 47. *Moralae Epistulae*, translated by R. M. Gummere, Loeb Classical Library (New York, 1917). All citations from the Epistles of Seneca are from this translation.

There is nothing in Stoicism to correspond to the keenness of expectation which colors Paul's views on the problems of marriage and slavery. The *status quo* is to be preserved. "This is what I appoint in all the churches" (I Cor. 7:17). He writes:

If a man was circumcised when he was called, let him not efface it. If he was uncircumcised, let him not be circumcised (I Cor. 7:18).

For the rest of the time those who have wives should live as though they had none, and those who mourn as though they did not mourn, and those who rejoice as though they did not rejoice, and those who buy anything as though they did not possess it, and those who mingle in the world as though they were not taken up with it (I Cor. 7:29-31).

In general, in these common social problems on which Paul pronounces an ethical judgment, we see no one norm set up, although there are two factors which seem to condition what he has to say: first, his confident expectation of the near end of the age, with the accompanying idea of reward and punishment, although the latter is not much stressed; and second, his mysticism which is based upon his spiritistic beliefs. For the most part he is content to work out the situation in the way that seems best at the moment, and in the way that secures the social approval of the people with whom he is working. The notable exception to the latter is the way he deals with the hostile group in the church. The trouble which arises at this point is due, in part at least, to the similarity of their respective approaches. Neither will allow the validity of the *gnosis* of the other.

§3

Another of the difficult problems with which Paul had to deal in Corinth was the matter of participation in pagan social and religious life. Corinth and its environs were well supplied with temples. In the city itself was a temple to Artemis of Ephesus; on the public square was a statue of Athena, a temple to Octavia, the sister of Augustus, and a temple to Zeus Capitolinus. On the way to Acro-Corinth there were important temples, among them those of Isis and Serapis, one erected to the Great Mother, and the famous temple of Aphrodite. If Strabo is correct about the thousand prostitutes of this temple,[11] the Jews were justified in connecting idolatry and immorality. Aphrodite had had an unenviable reputation with moralists for centuries. Antisthenes, the Cynic teacher, is said to have remarked that if he could get hold of Aphrodite he would shoot her.[12]

The group of Corinthian Christians who stressed *gnosis* saw no reason why they should not continue to enjoy these religious contacts, since idols were nonexistent anyway. They were in no mood to give up the pagan festivals which they enjoyed or to refuse invitations to dinner in the temple court or to cease visiting their old friends. Attending a meal in the court of a pagan temple was a matter of pure indifference, so far as any real danger was concerned. The possession of *gnosis* was the key to full freedom. Their attitude toward sex-relations and Paul's answer have already been noted.

Paul uses an Old Testament story to prove that even though the Israelites had the sacraments of Baptism and

[11] Strabo viii. 6.20.
[12] Clement of Alexandria, *Stromateis* ii.20, cited by A. C. Pearson, "Ethics and Morality" (Greek) *Encyclopedia of Religion and Ethics* (New York, 1919), V, 490.

the Eucharist in the wilderness, they had fallen twenty-three thousand in one day, as the result of yielding to idolatry and its accompanying immorality. The sacraments are not talismans—"The man who thinks he can stand must watch out lest he fall" (I Cor. 10:12).

Paul has much in common with these radical Christians of Corinth. He has long since ceased to observe the ceremonial law (cf. Gal. 2:1 ff.). He tells the Corinthians that they may eat what their pagan hosts in private homes set before them unless it is specifically stated that the meat had been offered in pagan sacrifice, when for the sake of the scruples of the "weak" Christians they should desist. His attitude comes out even more clearly in Rom. 14:14-23, which follows:

I know and am persuaded in the Lord Jesus that nothing is unclean in itself; a thing is unclean only to the person who believes it is unclean. For if your brother is grieved on account of food, you are not walking in love. Through food you must not ruin a man for whom Christ died. Do not, therefore, let your good be spoken of as evil. For the kingdom of God is not food and drink, but righteousness and peace and joy through the Holy Spirit. For he who serves Christ in this way is pleasing to God and approved by men. Let us therefore seek after the things of peace and for whatever contributes to our improvement. Do not merely for the sake of the food ruin the work of God. All things are clean, but it is wrong for a man to become a cause of offense by eating. It is good not to eat meat nor to drink wine if by doing so, you make your brother take offense. You must keep your faith a matter between yourself and God. Happy is he who does not condemn himself in what he approves. He who hesitates and then eats, is condemned because what he did was not from faith. Everything which is not from faith is wrong.

Paul is consistent in his position in the two letters, and he is on common ground with the Corinthian Christians

COMMUNITY PROBLEMS IN CORINTH

who were standing for freedom, but the radicals do not see the necessity of troubling themselves about the scruples of the "weak." "Why should my freedom be determined by another's conscience? If I partake of food with thanks, why should I be condemned for eating what I have given thanks for" (I Cor. 10:30)? This seems to imply a talismanic significance to "grace before meat" which is in line with the sacramental outlook.

Paul uses the same motivation in what he has to say about the Christians' eating in a pagan temple. They rightly see that the idol has no real existence, in spite of the many gods and lords. But the conscientious Christian, seeing his fellow-Christian eating here, will do the same, even though he still associates this with the idol as formerly. Then the realization that he has participated in pagan sacrifice will trouble his sensitive conscience. He is doing what his conscience condemns, which will mean his moral ruin. The right way is to avoid wounding the sensitive conscience of a weak brother. Paul is not individualistic here in his ethical outlook. Brother-love is placed above selfish insistence upon rights.

We are permitted to do anything, but everything is not to our advantage. We are permitted to do anything but not everything is constructive. Let no one seek his own advantage, but the advantage of others (I Cor. 10:23-24).

Paul's really clinching argument against participation in pagan festivals is the spiritistic one. The idol, it is true, does not exist, but the demon behind the idol is a reality.

What the Gentiles sacrifice they offer to demons and not to God, and I do not want you in fellowship with demons. You cannot drink the cup of the Lord and the cup of demons. You cannot share the table of the Lord and the table of demons. Or are we trying to move the Lord to jealousy? We are not stronger than he is, are we (I Cor. 10:20-22)?

The pagan cult meal and the Christian cult meal are mutually exclusive though both are clearly of sacramental significance. The Christian shares the blood and body of Christ. The participant in the pagan cult will most certainly take a demon inside him, which will drive out the *pneuma*, for Christ will not inhabit the same abode as a demon. Paul is here appealing to the instinct for self-preservation. In another context he implies that certain illnesses and deaths have resulted from wrong participation in the Eucharist (I Cor. 11:30).

The ethical motivation here is badly mixed. Paul uses two mutually exclusive lines of approach, the ethical and the sacramental, in appealing to the same group. In the attempt to penetrate behind Paul's words on the subject to the underlying social situation, we receive a little light on the problem. We can readily understand why Christians kept on accepting invitations to meals in pagan homes and continued to go to pagan festivals. The former Paul accepts because there is no other way out; so he urges respect for the scruples of the weak brother. This is plainly an ethical socially-conditioned argument. The attendance upon and participation in pagan cult meals is a different matter. He dare not compromise here. His reaction is Jewish. He sees "idolatry and immorality" together and trembles for his "saints." His real horror of immorality and his firm belief in demon control help to account for what he says. Paul's words in another connection, "I have become all things to all men, if by any means I may save some" (I Cor. 9:22b) apply to his ethical motivation in this problem when he mingles ethical

COMMUNITY PROBLEMS IN CORINTH 93

and sacramental arguments to prove his point and does it with greater calmness than is characteristic of him in other like situations.

§4

Paul faced certain practical problems in connection with the Christian meetings. What place were women to have in the cult meetings? How was the service of the Lord's Supper to be conducted? What provision is to be made for the orderly control of the so-called "spiritual gifts" *(charismata)*? His approach to these problems is of significance in the attempt to determine his ethical outlook.

There are two rules that Paul insists upon in connection with women in church, both of which are in logical contradiction with one of the most fundamental tenets of his religious outlook. He can say:

Yet in the Lord woman is neither separate from man, nor man from woman (I Cor. 11:11).

There can be no Jew nor Greek, no slave nor freeman, no male nor female, for in Christ you are all one (Gal. 3:28).

He can also say:

... woman is the reflection of man's glory. ... Man was not created for woman but woman for man. For this reason a woman ought to have the sign of her subjection on her head, even if only on account of the angels (I Cor. 11:9-10).

Women are to be silent in church, for they are not permitted to speak, but are to be in subjection even as the Law says. If they want to learn anything let them ask their own husbands at home, for it is a shame for a woman to speak in church (I Cor. 14:34-35).

A situation arises in Corinth that causes Paul to insist upon different conduct from what his theory would seem to allow. Women must be veiled in Christian meeting. In the first instance Paul seems to allow women to pray and to "prophesy" (I Cor. 11:5), while in the second (I Cor. 14:34) silence is insisted upon, apparently in the same kind of meeting, although the second passage is in the context relating to the conduct of Christian meetings and the procedure to be followed in the exercise of the "gifts" (*charismata*). When he limited the speaking "in a tongue" to two or three and that only if an interpreter were present, he informed the Christians that the rest must talk to themselves or to God. He is even more drastic in the limitation he puts on the women of the group.

Paul makes short shrift of any potential contentiousness with his "I recognize no other practice in worship than this, and neither do the churches of God" (I Cor. 11:16). And the second dictum is supported by an appeal to the Law (I Cor. 14:34) In each case the appeal is to an external authority, in the one case custom, in the other revelation. Why this was the custom in the churches is not stated. Jewish women were not compelled to be veiled during attendance at the synagogue services. They might take part as one of the seven in the reading of the Sabbath lessons, though this was disapproved on grounds of propriety and no instance is reported.[13] There is the same note in Paul's "Judge for yourselves. Is it fitting for a woman to pray with her head uncovered" (I Cor. 11:13)? Paul's argument gives point to Weiss's statement that we do not know the Corinthian circumstances sufficiently exactly to understand fully Paul's motive and argument.[14] Admittedly it is difficult to see why he should mix a simple appeal to custom and precedent with a religious basis of

---

[13] G. F. Moore, *Judaism* (Cambridge, 1927), II, 131.
[14] Johannes Weiss, *Der Erster Korintherbrief* (Göttingen, 1910), p. 268.

woman's inferior position, or why he should equate the cutting of the hair, which was a symbol of grief, with wearing a veil, which he interprets as a sign of subjection, and especially necessary on account of the angels. The struggles of commentators with the passage reveal its logical difficulties.

Ancient custom has been explained in this way.[15] Married women ordinarily wore veils when they appeared in public, especially if they belonged to the middle classes. Prostitutes wore veils when they went to the temples of the gods. The Christian church now has both classes in it. Married women may have to sit next to slaves and former prostitutes. What shall be the norm? Shall the matrons lay aside the veil, or shall the one-time prostitute accept it? Evidently there were "emancipated" women in Corinth who were not wearing veils to the Christian meetings while the "respectable" ones did. Paul says all women *must* and appeals to the general practice in the churches.

Paul also appeals to the Law to justify his prohibition of women's speaking in Christian meeting (I Cor. 14:34). He has just been laying down certain rules for procedure in the conduct of the meetings and supports them by stating that they are *commands of the Lord,* that is, as spiritistically mediated. If any one disregards these he is to be ignored. Paul uses the Law when it is convenient to do so, rejecting it as freely, since it is not a means of salvation. In very few situations, however, is Paul's heritage from Judaism so clear as in this one. His emotional reaction strongly conditions his judgment here. The attitude of late Judaism on women is revealed by Sirach, who wrote in the second century B.C. Ecclesiasticus 9:1-9 is instructive. Woman is a thoroughly unsafe object in society.

[15] *Ibid.,* pp. 268-269.

Be not jealous over the wife of thy bosom,
And teach her not an evil lesson against thyself.
Give not thy soul to a woman, That she should set
    her foot against thy strength.
Go not to meet a woman that playeth the harlot,
Lest haply thou fall into her snares.
Use not the company of a woman that is a singer
Lest haply thou be caught in her attempts.
Gaze not upon a maid, lest haply thou be trapped in
    her penalties.
Give not thy soul unto harlots,
That thou lose not thine inheritance.
Look not around thee in the streets of the city
Neither wander thou in the solitary places thereof.
Turn away thine eye from a comely woman,
And gaze not on another's beauty.
By the beauty of a woman many have been led astray;
And herewith love is kindled as a fire.
Sit not at all with a woman that hath a husband
And revel not with her at the wine.
Lest haply thy soul turn aside unto her,
And with the spirit thou slide into destruction.

Rabbi Jose B. Johanan of Jerusalem said, "Let thy house be opened wide; and let poor folk be thy household; and talk not much with the wife . . . so long as a man talks much with his wife, he causes evil to himself. . . ."[16]

Philo, Paul's contemporary, gives evidence that Diaspora Judaism was of the same opinion on the subject. He evidently had a model wife, for she wore no jewels and is said to have remarked, "The virtue of a husband is a suffi-

---

[16] *Pirke Aboth* i.5. Translated by R. T. Herford in *Apocrypha and Pseudepigrapha of the Old Testament*, edited by R. H. Charles (Oxford, 1913).

COMMUNITY PROBLEMS IN CORINTH 97

cient ornament for his wife."[17] The Essenes, of whom Philo thinks highly, repudiated marriage:

... for no one of the Essenes ever marries a wife, because woman is a selfish creature and one addicted to jealousy in an immoderate degree, and terribly calculated to overturn the natural inclinations of a man, and to mislead him by her continual tricks, for she is always studying deceitful speeches and all other kinds of hypocrisy, like an actress on the stage, when she is alluring the eyes and ears of her husband, she proceeds to cajole his predominant mind after the servants have been deceived.[18]

Commenting on Genesis 3:9 Philo says:

The woman, being imperfect and depraved by nature, made the beginnings of sinning and prevaricating; but the man as being the more excellent and perfect creature, was the first to set the example of blushing, and of being ashamed, and indeed of every good feeling and action.[19]

All was not well in Alexandria any more than in Corinth, for Philo writes,

Woman's place is in the home, let her stay at home except for temple visits, and these not when the streets are full. If she hears foul language, let her stop her ears and run away....

But as it is now some women are advanced to such a pitch of shamelessness, as not only, though they are women to give vent to intemperate language and abuse among a crowd of men, but even to strike men and insult them, with hands practiced rather in works of the loom, and in spinning than in blows and assaults like wrestlers.[20]

Not only was woman unsafe for man in human society, but the Jews carried over the idea into their view of the

---

[17] Philo, *Fragments*. Translated by C. D. Yonge (London, 1885), IV, 275.
[18] *Ibid.*, p. 221.
[19] Philo, *Questions and Solutions*, IV, 306.
[20] Philo, *On Special Laws*, III, 345, 346.

supernatural realm, and later Jewish literature uses the motif of Gen. 6:1, which may have some bearing upon Paul's obscure remark about women wearing veils for the sake of the angels. Paul's attitude is easily understandable in the light of such opinions about women. This is not to underestimate the practical difficulties of the problem which he faced. It is merely to face the indubitable fact that Paul could not always endure the logic of his own positions. Theoretically, being *en Christō* was the point of fundamental importance; practically, it was of slight importance against Paul's inherited prejudices and the exigencies of the immediate situation.

The disorderly conduct at the supper-meeting which preceded the observance of the Lord's Supper has been noted. Paul flatly declares that their meetings are doing more harm than good (I Cor. 11:17). Sectarianism is present, disregard of the poor and hungry, and even drunkenness. Paul cannot approve of this kind of conduct (I Cor. 11:22). He appeals again to the tradition of a simple memorial meal, but he passes quickly to the sacramental conception of cult meals and states that wrong participation in the blood and body of the Lord is at the basis of certain illnesses and deaths which have occurred in the Christian community. Paul here, as elsewhere, reënforces Christian tradition by appeal to the spiritistic or sacramental (I Cor. 11:30).

The problem of the Christian meeting was the control of the "gifts." This has been described in Chapter II in connection with the religion of Paul. There remains the ethical element to consider here. There is no doubt that Paul valued the "gifts" highly. He thanks God he can speak ecstatically (I Cor. 14:18), boasts of "visions and revelations" (II Cor. 12:1-6), and urges the community

COMMUNITY PROBLEMS IN CORINTH

to cultivate the "higher endowments" (I Cor. 14:1), to set their hearts upon being inspired to preach (i.e., "to prophesy"), even while putting no hindrance in the way of ecstasy (I Cor. 14:39). The spiritistic side of Paul's religion is never more in evidence than in these three chapters (I Cor. 12-14), yet the chief impression is the ethical one. He would not use his gift of ecstasy individualistically; he would rather speak five words with his understanding that would help others than ten thousand in a tongue. He would prefer to have the Corinthians value him on the basis of his conduct rather than because he has had wonderful visions and revelations (II Cor. 12:6). The "gifts" are for the common good; the "body of the Lord" (i.e., the Christian group) should function as the human body does, in perfect coördination, and not with any part jealous of another part. This emphasis on the group is not Hellenistic, but Jewish, and here we see the blend of the major influences that played upon Paul. Paul can reject the Jewish means of acquittal, he can rejoice in the emotional approach to religion, but he cannot give way to the idea of unrestrained individualism in religion.

It is out of this emphasis upon the common good which characterized Paul's outlook that we have the well-known hymn of love, I Corinthians, chapter 13. It takes on an added significance when it is oriented into the living situation out of which it issued. There is clear evidence that Paul is thinking of the Christians who are hostile to him, and yet the note of personal bitterness is lacking. He has already reminded them (I Cor. 8:1 ff.) that love is superior to the *gnosis* in which they take such satisfaction. He would again remind them of its absolute supremacy among "spiritual" gifts. These gifts which they and he prize so highly are transitory; only love is permanent.

Prophesying, ecstatic speaking, *gnosis* are all temporary, destined to pass away (I Cor. 13:8). Speaking in a tongue, either of men or of angels, without love is like the noisy clashing of gongs and cymbals that are part of the accessories of the mystery cults. Even the "prophesying" of secret truths known only to the initiated, and the possession of all *gnosis* without love are as nothing. A man may renounce all his property, be willing for martyrdom itself, but if love is lacking, his sacrificial acts are of no value. The beautiful verses 4-7 show what the Corinthian Christians or at least a group of them lack. They are the opposite of these attributes.

Love is patient and kind, it is not envious, it does not boast, it is not puffed up with pride. It does not behave dishonorably, it is not self-seeking, it is not roused to anger, it does not think evil, it does not rejoice in wickedness, but rejoices only in truth. It will bear anything, believe anything, hope for anything, endure anything.

Lietzmann sees in this song of love the most brilliant piece of evidence for the justification of the world-historical significance of the Apostle Paul because it gives the deepest glimpse into the essence of his religion. He sees in Paul a real ancient who was molded by Greek and Jewish influence, but who, in spite of that, grasped with full clearness the religious value of the religion of Jesus and saw it as the heart and goal of the Christian life. It is perhaps the highest reach of Paul's thought, and no picture of him would be complete without full recognition of the heights to which he could ascend. Paul is at his best ethically in this section (I Cor. 12-14).

It has been noted from time to time that Paul employs the terminology of the mystery cults. The researches of Professor Richard Reitzenstein have established this fact.

Even the scholars who are not sympathetic to the Hellenistic affiliations of early Christianity admit the use of Hellenistic terms, while insisting that the content is original with Paul, or if not original at least derived from Jesus or from Judaism. Lietzmann, as just indicated, finds the real origin of the hymn of love in the fact that Paul grasped the religion of Jesus most clearly. Is Chapter 13, then, to be lifted out of its Hellenistic setting of spiritism and treated as a thing apart? It has its Hellenistic connections. Paul ends this great exposition of love with the statement: "Faith, hope and love endure. These three, and the greatest of these is love." This formula or triad is the only one in Paul's genuine writings. Reitzenstein shows that Paul found a formula of four members: faith, hope, love, knowledge, and in the light of the overemphasis of the latter, struck it out and kept the other three members. The basis of this judgment is the presence of Hellenistic parallels.[21]

Whatever its origin, this great chapter is convincing evidence that while Paul's ethics is often religiously based, the distinctive emphasis in his religion, spiritism, is in this fine setting ethically based.

[21] Reitzenstein, *op. cit.*, pp. 383-93, treats of I Cor. 13. Philo is witness to the use of three and four-membered formulae, one of which is *pistis, chara, orasis* (synonymous with *gnosis*). He believes that the original source is Persian mysticism, and that Paul changed the formula in his fight with *gnosis* as it expressed itself among a part of the Christians at Corinth.

CHAPTER IV

WAS PAUL AN INTELLECTUAL?

WAS Paul primarily an intellectual? What are his claims to a place among the *literati* of the first century? What constituted intellectualism in this period? Do the writings of Paul show affinities with those of the philosophers of the Hellenistic period? Is the influence of Hellenism upon Paul found in the area of philosophical thought or of religious practice? These questions have not been answered with any approach to agreement.

Although Paul himself disclaims any desire to use the philosophical approach (I Cor. 2:1-5) and scorns the "pretensions of philosophy" (Col. 2:8 ff.), certain scholars have put him among those deeply influenced by Stoic intellectualism. Others deny any influence outside Judaism and his own personal experience, and still others see him influenced by Hellenism outside the range of philosophical speculation. Protestant scholars have often considered him the great early Christian intellectual, a theologian par excellence. In any attempt to discover the origin of Paul's ethical teaching, account must be taken of the thought of the period, especially as it found expression in Stoicism with its outstanding emphasis upon ethics.

§ 1

First-century intellectualism is a complex phenomenon, although for practical purposes it is subsumed under Rom-

WAS PAUL AN INTELLECTUAL? 103

anized Stoicism with some attention to the rival school, Epicureanism. The latter, however, seems to have had no influence upon early Christianity.

Stoicism in the Roman period may be studied in the writings of Cicero, Seneca, Epictetus and Marcus Aurelius. As a system Stoicism stood for five hundred years, which shows its essential adaptability to changing situations. The Roman world took over Stoicism from the Greeks, although it is not of Greek but rather of oriental origin. It is the intellectual descendant of the older movement, Cynicism, whose founder was Antisthenes, a contemporary of Plato. The older Cynics, notably Antisthenes and Diogenes, represent a revolt from the speculation current in the fourth century B.C., that brilliant period characterized by the influence of the great idealist, Plato, and the equally great empiricist, Aristotle. Certain of the Cynics, particularly Diogenes, scorned all civilized conventions to the point of being anti-social. Stoicism, even in its earlier, more austere form, did much to tone down the harshness of the older Cynic school. While it did not neglect such speculative subjects as logic and physics, its main concern was ethics, which Stoics considered the noblest type of philosophy. It is even stated that both the leading schools of the fourth century B.C., Epicureanism and Stoicism, belong quite as much to the history of religion as to the history of philosophy.

It is no accident that Stoicism's main concern was with moral and religious problems. This concern was the result of social experience. In the breakdown of the old type of political organization following the conquests of Alexander, old thought-forms and old religious securities did not give the help that struggling, discouraged, fearful individuals needed. There was demand for outside help.

Stoicism and the mystery cults attempted to meet that demand. As has been indicated, Cynicism was the ancestor of Stoicism. We have a description of the work of the Cynic preacher.

Long before the Christian preacher bore his new message through the world, pagan preachers wandered over the same roads bringing a message to mankind. In the horrors of chaos of the early Hellenistic period, in a society struggling out of the ruins of the past to a new life, a society distressed by the terrors of the past and by the uncertainties of the future, the Cynic preachers first found fruitful soil for their mission, and the popular preaching, freed from the early crude forms, could represent the better knowledge and the higher ideal to a humanity foundering in low-thinking enjoyment of life and in ethical deterioration. These preachers feel themselves the divinely sent messengers whom humanity has to observe and respect, as doctors whom sick mankind must accept.[1]

A deep concern with ethics was Stoicism's heritage from its past.

To understand fully the Stoicism of Paul's day, the contribution of Posidonius to its formulation must be noted. He has been ranked as the most important figure after Aristotle until Neo-Platonism. Paul Wendland, one of the most able students of Graeco-Roman culture, pronounces the system of the Stoic Posidonius "the last great creation of the Greek spirit." In him were united a deep historical sense and ability for exact investigation, speculative power and religious feeling. He is credited with giving a new direction to Stoicism, with exerting a strong influence upon Neo-Pythagoreanism and Platonism, with influencing early Christian literature through the medium of Philo. Hans Böhlig in his excellent study, *Die Geistes-*

---

[1] Paul Wendland, *Die Hellenistisch-Römische Kultur* (Tübingen, 1912), pp. 81-82.

kultur von Tarsos, claims that Posidonius stamped the philosophy of Tarsus. His importance lies also in his certain position as the representative of the beginning of the eclectic tendency in Greek philosophy, the tendency to combine. This results in a syncretism, the inevitable consequence of which is to vulgarize philosophy. This new departure is dated at about 100 B.C. and Posidonius is named as the most prominent of the Stoics who *Platonized*. His influence can be clearly seen in the *Hermetica*, described as "those Greek and Latin writings which contain religious or philosophic teaching ascribed to Hermes Trismegistus." Edwyn Bevan sees his significance in his ability to group, more completely than any other person had done, the mass of beliefs which haunted the spirits of men and to give them more eloquent and appealing form. Cicero and Philo stand out as writers of eclectic tendency. Plutarch does also, although he was more of an essayist than a philosopher.

Posidonius brought mysticism and astrology into Stoicism. Mysticism was part of a larger movement dating from the sixth century B.C. Such tendencies as those represented by Orphics, Pythagoreans, and Platonists are part of a larger whole. In the sphere of astrology Posidonius is truly the agent of syncretism between East and West. In the words of Cumont:

But the scholar whose authority contributes most to the final acceptance of sidereal divination was a Syrian philosopher of encyclopedic knowledge, Posidonius of Apamea, the teacher of Cicero. The works of that erudite and religious writer influenced the development of the entire Roman theology more than anything else.[2]

[2] Franz Cumont, *Oriental Religions in Roman Paganism* (Chicago, 1911), p. 164.

Sidereal religion was first received in the upper classes, and then was propagated among the masses by the clergy and devotees of the mystery cults. It transformed the deities of these cults. Attis became a solar deity; Mithra became *Sol Invictus*. Astrology became divinely revealed doctrine instead of a theory of mathematicians. The triumph of oriental religions was at the same time the triumph of astral religion. The Stoics supported astrology.

It is difficult for a modern mind to conceive of astrology as forming a part of intellectualism. If we set up Aristotle as the norm of ancient intellectualism and the modern scientist as that of modern intellectualism, we are obliged to admit that first-century intellectualism was far from intellectual. But to set up such norms is what we may not do. Rather we must be descriptive and not dogmatic upon what constitutes intellectualism in the first century. Cumont says of Posidonius:

Brought up on Plato and Aristotle, he was equally versed in Asiatic astrology and demonology. More of a theologian than a philosopher, in mind more learned than critical, he made all human knowledge conspire to the building up of a great system the coping of which was the enthusiastic adoration of the God who penetrates the universal organism. In this vast syncretism all superstition, popular or sacerdotal, sooth-saying, divination, magic find their place and their justification, but above all it was due to him that astrology entered into a coherent explanation of the world, acceptable to the most enlightened intellects, and that it was solidly based on a general theory of nature from which it was to remain henceforth inseparable.[3]

The most dangerous by-product of this religion was the idea of fatalism which it imposed upon the ancient world. The Chaldeans were the first to conceive the idea

[3] From Cumont, *Astrology and Religion Among the Greeks and Romans* (New York, 1912), p. 84. Courtesy of G. P. Putnam's Sons, New York and London.

WAS PAUL AN INTELLECTUAL? 107

of necessity dominating the universe. This comes to be a Stoic idea, too. Fatalism is a theory of despair, crushing to the spirit of man, and sure to result in the practice of exorcism. Oriental religions gained popularity by their ability along this line. They guaranteed to the individual a blessed immortality which would compensate for the fears and anxieties of the present life. It would really seem that Epicureanism was the only intellectual movement of this period that keep its head in control. Its thoroughly materialistic outlook kept it from being able to take refuge in mysticism. Its insistence upon getting rid of fear kept astrology and its accompanying fatalism from getting the upper hand over the minds of Epicureans.

It is not surprising, in the light of this background, that Gilbert Murray describes the spirit of the Hellenistic age of philosophy in these words:

It is hard to describe. It is a rise of asceticism, of mysticism, in a sense of pessimism, a loss of self-confidence, of hope in this life and of faith in normal human effort; a despair of patient inquiry, a cry for infallible revelation, an indifference to the welfare of the state, a conversion of the soul to God. It is an atmosphere in which the aim of the good man is not so much to live justly, to help the society to which he belongs, to enjoy the esteem of his fellow-creatures; but rather by means of a burning faith, by contempt for the world and its standards, by ecstasy, suffering and martyrdom, to be granted pardon for his unspeakable unworthiness, his immeasurable sins. There is an intensifying of certain spiritual emotions, an increase of sensitiveness, a failure of nerve.[4]

In the Christian church at Colossae there were practices that link up with this general spirit of the time somewhat more closely than do those of the churches described in

[4] Reprinted from Murray, *Five Stages of Greek Religion*, p. 155, with the permission of Columbia University Press.

the other Pauline letters. In this letter there is evidence that points to syncretism. Paul talks about the "pretensions of philosophy," which to him is mere human tradition. Mysticism is present, and also the worship of angels (Col. 2:18). There is the tendency to asceticism which Paul deplores (Col. 2:20-23). There is evidence of the influence of Judaism in this situation (Col. 2:16), as well as of Gnosticism. The Christians have been freed from the "elements" *(stoicheia)* through the death of Christ, an act of cosmic significance (Col. 2:15). What we see as "philosophy" in the Colossian situation may belong to first-century intellectualism, but it does not belong to the line of approach of a Cicero, a Seneca, an Epictetus, or a Plutarch.

The definitions of the "philosophy" of Colossae are as variant as the elements comprising the religious syncretism of the period. To one it is "a gnostic religion of self-redemption with a Jewish foundation"; to another it is a worship of angels closely related to the mystery cults. Cosmological speculation constituted the center of Paul's fight at Colossae, while a third writer sees in the situation an attempt to intellectualize the Colossian Christianity by making it into a superior philosophy. These Colossian religionists would assume to complete the revelation. Paul fought their claims because their system of hierarchies diminished Jesus by reducing him to one in a hierarchy, one of the redeemers but not the unique and only redeemer. Hence Paul's argument on the sufficiency of Christ.

§ 2

First-century intellectualism has been synonymous with Stoicism in the minds of the writers about Paul and his relation to the thought of the age. As early as 1868

WAS PAUL AN INTELLECTUAL? 109

the eminent Cambridge scholar, J. B. Lightfoot, wrote a dissertation on Paul and Seneca. His essay is a valuable source for Stoic parallels to New Testament language. In brief compass he presents the sayings of Seneca that have linguistic affinity with those of the New Testament writers. The author warns against taking the coincidence of language too seriously. The same word may not mean the same thing to Paul and to Seneca. He expresses amazement that early Christian writers could have thought of Seneca as Christian after reading even a few pages of his writing. He makes one statement to which we shall have occasion to recur: "It is difficult to estimate and perhaps not very easy to overrate the extent to which Stoic philosophy had leavened the moral vocabulary of the civilized world at the time of the Christian era."[5]

Another Cambridge scholar, E. V. Arnold, writing more recently, also warns against too much stress on parallels of phrases used by Christian and Stoic writers. His reason for caution is that many parallels can be traced to common sources from which each religion drew in turn, as, for example, Persian thought, from which the Stoics inherited through Heraclitus, and Christianity through Judaism. He further notes that individuals in either camp were influenced by the same *zeitgeist* which has been described in this chapter.[6] He finds Stoic influence on Paul in the sphere of metaphysics, in his idea of the universe, of divine immanence, of human nature, of immortality,

[5] J. B. Lightfoot, "St. Paul and Seneca," *St. Paul's Epistle to the Philippians* (London, 1908), p. 303.

[6] E. V. Arnold, *Roman Stoicism* (Cambridge, 1911), p. 409. The concluding chapter, "The Stoic Strain in Christianity," is disappointing so far as Paul is concerned. One feels that the author has done well to admit in a footnote that he had applied no critical theories to his interpretation of the New Testament. He uses the speeches in Acts as Pauline, and often groups Paul and his successors together as Paulists, with no very clear demarcation between them.

and of moral principles. Most of these assertions could be easily contested. Bonhöffer's judgment that he has overrated the Stoic influence on Paul seems to the present writer to be well taken.

The most thorough study of Paul's relation to Stoicism has been worked out in Adolf Bonhöffer's *Epiktet und das Neue Testament*. Bonhöffer's contemporaries were inclined to find much in Paul that was taken over out of Stoic popular philosophy. He examines forty-eight words of special significance that Paul has in common with Epictetus and believes that he has shown that they do not betray an especially close relationship of the apostle with the secular literature or with the thought-forms and modes of expression of the Greeks. They are almost all words which have come to him out of the Septuagint, especially out of the Old Testament apocrypha.

He next examines the style of the apostle and finds that the idea of dependence upon the Cynic-Stoic diatribe has been exaggerated, in that its use is not general, being almost absent in the Corinthian correspondence. Furthermore, even in the letters where it is present it is only in parts of those letters, i.e., in the polemical or the dogmatic parts. It should be noted that Bonhöffer does not deny influence from contemporary modes of speech, but only literary dependence upon the Cynic-Stoic diatribe. He admits similarity in the method of argumentation between Paul and Epictetus, but this is not an evidence of the influence of Greek rhetoric in a literary way. Rather he sees Judaism accounting for everything which cannot be explained out of the conversion and subsequent Christian experience. Paul's spirit is totally different from that of the Stoics.

Two of Bonhöffer's contemporaries are at variance

WAS PAUL AN INTELLECTUAL? 111

with his conclusions. Rudolf Bultmann had found the contribution of the Stoics to be more considerable than Bonhöffer will allow. Hans Böhlig makes one major criticism. He denies the right to attempt to fit Paul into a rigid Stoic scheme, which does not take into account the Middle Stoa, particularly Posidonius, and then to decide that because Paul does not fit into such a scheme the Stoic influence upon him was nil. Similarly, Böhlig's own conclusion is that Stoic influence was slight, and that what there was, was mediated through the Judaism of Tarsus, with the exception of the idea of "conscience" *(suneidesis)*. This idea, he held, was appropriated more directly and then remodelled.[7]

In his *Der Stil der Paulinischen Predigt* Rudolf Bultmann has made a valuable contribution to the literature of Stoic influence on Paul. He finds that influence in those parts of Paul's letters that have the closest relation to oral discourse and concludes that Paul's *preaching* was in the style of the Cynic-Stoic popular preachers. Bultmann considers this fact significant because it points to the fact of two different spiritual forces working at the same time and on the same soil and using similar forms of expression. He sees Paul's dependence on the diatribe, but he expresses it in this fashion: "The mantle of the Greek orators hangs on the shoulders of Paul, but Paul had no taste for artistically correct drapery, and the lines of an alien figure shine through everywhere."[8]

Bultmann sees in Paul's use of this contemporary form of expression an important means of contact with the folk, who would see in it the familiar, while what was not

[7] Hans Böhlig, *Die Geistes-kultur von Tarsos* (Göttingen, 1913), p. 168. For his criticism of Bonhöffer see p. 128.

[8] Rudolf Bultmann, *Der Stil der Paulinischen Predigt* (Göttingen, 1910), p. 108. The section, pp. 107-9, is interesting.

familiar would take on the attractiveness of the exotic. He sees Paul, not only as using the same medium of expression, but also as similar in spirit. The diatribe becomes the means of clarifying and enfolding his own spiritual possession. Indeed Bultmann is willing to see Paul appropriating, not only the form, but the content of the contemporary preachers, and in the instances of his conceptions of freedom and slavery he see Paul reflecting contemporary attitudes. This, however, is a debatable question, as Paul's statements can be motivated otherwise in each case with equal authentication. The investigation of form and content belong together, and Bultmann thinks that this has bearing upon the genuineness of Paul's writings, and that the form is a means of control for the investigation of other problems.

Böhlig and Bonhöffer find Stoic influence slight. Bultmann sees in it a very vital significance, particularly in the area of method. Chappuis, a French scholar writing as recently as 1926, presents a chapter on Paul and Stoicism that all but makes Paul a Stoic. No other influence is comparable to that of Stoicism. This author delights in metaphysics and is not at all in sympathy with the more recent approaches to the study of ethics. His attitude is expressed in the following: "No philosophical school has ever divorced morality from metaphysics. Practical philosophy is vivified and sustained by metaphysical speculation."[9] This conviction sets the tone of his study of Paul. Paul was devoted to moral problems; therefore, he must have had a metaphysical background. What is more natural than to search Paul for evidence of connection with Stoicism, the one philosophical school of prominence in his day?

[9] Paul Chappuis, *La Destinée de L'Homme* (Paris, 1926), p. 52. Pp. 34-51 are devoted to Paul.

WAS PAUL AN INTELLECTUAL? 113

The areas in which Chappuis finds Stoic metaphysics in Paul are: the idea of divine causality, the metaphysical character of Christ, and the general conception of God. The fire of the *Parousia* is Stoic eschatology; the spiritual body of I Corinthians, chapter 15 is incomprehensible apart from the Stoic idea of the corporeality of the soul. Finally Paul's letters echo that common maxim of the Stoics, "live according to nature." This author seems to be utterly unacquainted with the connection of Paul with the less intellectualistic phases of the Greek world. Paul must be made a metaphysician because he is concerned with ethics, and there can be no practical concern with ethics without an accompanying metaphysics. Paul, therefore, is forced into the Stoic scheme with a rigidity seldom found even in those writers who take extremist positions. The chapter is interesting as an example of the century-long search for evidence to make Paul an intellectual of the intellectuals, but it does not depict a busy missionary working to render comprehensible a message of supreme concern to him, nor does this author seem to understand how Paul met problems in groups whose members would not know one metaphysical concept from another.

§ 3

Was Paul an intellectual? The foregoing survey of scholarly opinion shows that there is a wide divergence on this question. Paul's own letters should be the final court of appeal. If his approach to life and its problems is similar to the Stoic approach, it should be in evidence here. We have been duly warned of the unwisdom of taking coincidences of language too seriously. It is sound historical method to set forth the major emphases of Paul and see if they are also of major concern to the intellectuals of his day, so far as we can discover those interests in their extant literary remains. Paul dealt with practical problems; so did the Stoics. There should be points of contact here. There are certain interests of the Pauline churches that are quite outside the ken of Stoic intellectuals. Paul therefore writes on a number of subjects which we may at once eliminate as of no concern to the Stoics. They are: his whole concern with the problem of circumcision and observance of the Law of Moses, the imminent *Parousia* and the Resurrection; the eating of meat which had been offered in pagan sacrifice; all problems arising in connection with the Christian sacraments of Baptism and the Eucharist. Here are areas of interest to Paul that have no connection whatever with first-century intellectualism.

Under any rigid adherence to chronology Epictetus and Plutarch would be ruled out as representative intellectuals to be compared with Paul, since they wrote from the end of the first Christian century. Our purpose, however, does not demand such rigidity. The major interests of first-century intellectuals, whatever the exact period of their lives, are of concern to us, as we seek Paul's intellectual interests. Plutarch is not so pronounced a Stoic as either Seneca or Epictetus since Mahaffy can say of him that "it would be hard to say whether the number of Stoic dogmas which he rejects exceeds the number which he quotes with approval."[10] He is a distinguished representative of that first-century movement which ultimately issued in Neo-Platonism, which certainly ranks him among the intellectuals. Emerson has some interesting phrases describing him: "an encyclopedia of Greek and Roman

[10] J. P. Mahaffy, *The Greek World Under Roman Sway* (London, 1890), p. 301.

antiquity," "a compend of all accepted traditions," "a master of ancient culture," "a chief example of the illumination of the intellect by the force of morals." He further says that Plutarch gossips of heroes, philosophers and poets, of virtues and genius, of love and fate and empires and that he "prattles history." To representatives of an age of specialization he will appear superficial, because the range of his interests is so wide. One needs but recall his production of forty-six biographies and sixty essays to realize the truth of that judgment even as one marks its modern bias.

On the other hand, it is well to realize that along with extant pictures of first-century morals that reveal extreme laxity, there is the other side in the picture of Plutarch's virtuous man.[11] He is a good father and brother, and a loyal friend. He is moderate in his pleasures, he strikes the golden mean between miserliness and extravagance. He is not an extremist who avoids the reasonable satisfaction of natural desires. He is always courteous, and while not a pedant, is a lover of all good learning. "Such a state of moral health," observes Rose, "is not to be reached in a moment, but is the ripe fruit of training and self-discipline." Plutarch's essays bring the reader into the presence of a genial, kindly, humane person, who steers a safe middle course and holds fast to what he believes to be good. He was a model of propriety, a veritable social mentor, the most pleasing portrait of the cultured gentleman of the first century of the Christian era that has been preserved.

There are a few points on which we have the views of both Paul and the intellectuals of his day. They are marriage, immorality, slavery, and asceticism. We have shown

[11] H. J. Rose, *The Roman Questions of Plutarch* (Oxford, 1924), p. 61.

the similarity and contrast between Paul and Epictetus on the matter of marriage. We have compared Paul and Seneca for their attitudes on slavery. Epictetus' wrath, which he vented upon one of the *literati* of his day who was detected in adultery, has been cited. We have seen that Paul was very much the Jew in his attitudes toward women. Seneca cannot be said to believe in the equality of the sexes when he says that the one is born to command and the other to obey, in the same context with the admission that each contributes an equal share to human society.[12] He has, however, one statement that points to a single standard of sex morality as the fitting one. ". . . You know that a man does wrong in requiring chastity of his wife when he is intriguing with the wives of other men, you know that as your wife should have no dealings with a lover, neither should you yourself with a mistress, and yet you do not act accordingly."[13] In the epistle following he describes the similarity of conduct of men and women, pointing out that the vicious living in which the women of the day were indulging was bringing the same toll of disease that it did to men.

There is extant from the pen of Plutarch a series of advices to a bride and bridegroom under the title *Conjugal Precepts*, which is as interesting as it is inconsistent. It is a fine example of the difficulty of trying to be on both sides of the same question at the same time. For example, ". . . in a well-managed household everything is done by mutual consent, but the husband's supremacy is exhibited, and his wishes are consulted" (xi). The wife is to have no private emotions (xiv), no private friends (xix), and especially should she worship her husband's gods. In one

---
[12] Seneca *On the Firmness of the Wise Man* I. From *Minor Dialogues*. Translated by Aubrey Stewart, Bohn Classical Library (New York, 1910).

[13] Seneca *Epistle* 94.

WAS PAUL AN INTELLECTUAL? 117

context he says the wife should not be vexed at her husband's amours with courtesans or maid-servants, but consider "that it is out of respect to her that he bestows upon another all his wanton depravity" (xvi); while in another place he points out that husbands should be willing to forego the use of perfumes to which their wives object, and "since they suffer quite as much when their husbands go with other women it is unjust for a small pleasure to pain and grieve wives, and not to abstain from connection with other women . . ." (xliv). "And he who enjoys pleasures that he forbids his wife, is like the man that orders his wife to go on fighting against an enemy to whom he has himself surrendered" (xlvii). "For it is not possible to banish extravagance from the women's side of the house if it is always to be seen in the men's apartments" is also an indication of a single standard.

Plutarch approves of women's having a liberal education. He advises the young husband to teach his wife philosophy. Apparently Plutarch fears no evil effects of higher learning for women. "For such teaching in the first place detaches women from absurdities; for the woman who has learnt geometry will be ashamed to dance, nor will she believe in incantations and spells if she has been charmed by the discourses of Plato and Xenophon . . . for if they are not well-informed by good precepts, and share in the teaching that men get, they generate among themselves many foolish and absurd ideas and states of mind" (xlviii). Plutarch's own domestic relations seem to have been satisfactory if we may judge from his *Consolatory Letter to His Wife*.

Plutarch was too sociable, too urbane to be in sympathy with ascetic practices, except as they came in natural connection with his religious and priestly functions as a priest of Pythian Apollo at Charonea. His attitude toward Orphism was that of moderation. We have noted that Paul gives no countenance to ascetic practices (Col. 2:20-23), that he is out of sympathy with the ascetic ideal, but in sympathy with those who are not yet emancipated from it (Rom. 14). There is an ascetic element in Epictetus, when he can say, "What am I? A poor soul laden with a corpse."[14] And Seneca shows an ascetic tendency when he talks of the body in these terms:

For this body of ours is a weight upon the soul and its presence, as the load presses down the soul is crushed and is in bondage, unless philosophy has come to its assistance and has bid it take fresh courage by contemplating the universe, and has turned it from things earthy to things divine. . . .

I was born to a greater destiny than to be a mere chattel of my body, and I regard this body as nothing but a chain which manacles my freedom. . . . To despise our bodies is sure freedom.[15]

There is in Seneca a repugnance to the older Cynic ideal with its repellent asceticism and its anti-social habits, which he calls "perverted forms of self-display." Quoting the Stoic slogan "Live according to nature," he adds ". . . it is quite contrary to nature to torture the body, to hate unlabored elegance, to be dirty on purpose, to eat food that is not only plain, but disgusting and forbidding."[16] It should be noted that asceticism as Seneca depicts it is not the asceticism of the mysteries or of the Neo-Pythagoreans. It is not asceticism for the achievement of religious ends; there is neither fasting, lustrations, or initiation.

What were the major emphases of Paul? His own letters are our best source-material, particularly those sections where he is most spontaneous and therefore most

[14] Cited by Marcus Aurelius *Meditations* iv. 41.
[15] Seneca *Epistle* 65. [16] Seneca *Epistle* 5.

WAS PAUL AN INTELLECTUAL? 119

original, although the other sections are not to be ruled out. Indeed it is in the more stereotyped sections that we might expect to find the clearest traces of formulation that shows the previous adoption of much from current sources.

Paul's method of presenting the Christian message is allied with the mystery cults rather than with the intellectualism of his day. Twice he alludes to his method of approach: Gal. 3:1 and I Cor. 2:2 ff. This is a pictorial approach designed to appeal to the emotions, something that would have horrified a true Stoic, whose aim was to subdue the emotions, to live by reason and not by feeling. The method suited the Galatians and the Corinthians. Paul reports satisfactory results in both cases (Gal. 3:3-5; I Cor. 2:4; cf. II Cor. 12:12). We need not go beyond the bare statement that a Christian meeting such as is pictured in I Cor. 14:26-40 would have been quite outside the pale of Stoic propriety. Although Cicero states that no school of philosophers has made so many innovations as the Stoics, it is impossible to imagine a Cicero, a Seneca, an Epictetus, or a Plutarch participating in such a meeting.

The term "holy spirit" is common to Paul and Seneca, but the similarity does not go beyond language. Seneca says, "God is near you, he is within you ... a holy spirit dwells within us, one who marks our good and evil deeds and is our guardian."[17] Spirit *(pneuma)* to the Stoic was part of man's constitution as man, as Epictetus beautifully says, "We are fragments of God."[18] *Pneuma* was not with the Stoics as with Paul, something that came into certain men as a supernatural element that changed the constitution of their nature. Reitzenstein has pointed out, as we have noted in another connection, that Paul's use of the term is found also in the magical papyri, that he is there-

[17] Seneca *Epistle* 41.   [18] Epictetus *Discourses* ii. 8.

fore simply using the language of his time, and that his use of *pneuma* and *nous* in I Cor. 2:11 and 2:15-16 is similar to Oriental-hellenistic usage.

Paul's very common formula to be "in Christ" or to be "a new creation in Christ Jesus" has no counterpart in Stoicism. The Stoics had no Redeemer-god, no cult-Lord, such as Paul pictures in every letter. This is a fundamental tenet in Paul's religion. To bring men into union with the cult-Lord was Paul's mission in life. He was surer of nothing than that he had this desired union.

> I have been crucified with Christ. I no longer live but Christ lives in me. The life I now live in the body I live by faith in the Son of God who loved me and gave himself for me. I will not set aside the favor of God. For if acquittal could come through the Law, then Christ died in vain (Gal. 2:20-21).

This is not the language of Stoicism, even though Epictetus does allude to men as "sons of God."[19] God was not personal, nor was there a future judgment to escape by means of God's acquittal.

> So if anyone is in Christ he is a new creation. The old things have passed away, and there is a new state (II Cor. 5:17).

> Indeed I consider all things as loss when compared with the surpassing worth of the knowledge of Christ Jesus, my Lord. For whose sake I have lost everything, and count everything refuse, to the end that I may gain Christ and be found in him. . . . I would know him both in the power of his resurrection and the fellowship of his sufferings even to a similar death, if by that I might attain to the resurrection from among the dead (Phil. 3:8-11).

The Stoics prided themselves on their indifference to such external matters as property, and they have a good deal to

---

[19] Epictetus *Discourses* i. 9.

WAS PAUL AN INTELLECTUAL? 121

say about facing death calmly, but the tenor and content of the above have no counterpart in Stoicism.

One might add Romans 6:3-11; 8:1-2, 9b-11, 38 f., and still the list would not be exhaustive. These are all key passages to the understanding of Paul's religion. Paul's song of triumph would fit ill upon the lips of a Stoic philosopher:

For I am persuaded that neither death nor life, neither angels nor sovereignties, neither things present nor things to come, nor powers, nor heights nor depths will be able to separate us from the love of God which is in Christ Jesus our Lord (Rom. 8:38-39).

In the realm of mystery-cult and gnostic ideas Paul is quite outside the Stoic intellectualism of his day. The Stoic use of knowledge, according to Cicero, is that knowledge is to be acquired for its own sake, because it contains something which has embraced and seized upon truth.[20] Paul is in line with Hellenistic usage, which Wendland describes thus: "The Gnostics are not religious philosophers; Gnosticism is not knowledge that appeals to the understanding, but a vision of God, secret wisdom which is won through personal connection with God and through revelation."[21] Reitzenstein, too, insists that nothing is more mistaken than the attempt to explain *gnosis* as an early effort to formulate a Christian or a religious philosophy, thus unduly emphasizing theoretical elements. It should be noted that pre-Christian Gnosticism must be understood in the wider study of the history of religions, even if the more highly developed systems are to be connected with Christianity.

In Paul the gnostic and mystery terminologies run into

[20] Cicero *De Finibus* iii. 5. Translated by H. Rackham, Loeb Classical Library (New York, 1914).
[21] Wendland, *op. cit.*, p. 166.

each other. There are two places in Paul's letters where these types of terminology abound: I Cor. 2:6-16 and much of Colossians, chapters 1-2. It seems clear that Gnosticism cannot be called an intellectual movement until the second century with the development of the great systems, such as are described by Irenaeus in *Against Heresies*.

Paul speaks of preaching the "wisdom" of God when he is among the "initiated," the "wisdom of God in a mystery" which was predestined to redound to the glory of Christians. These secret truths of God are revealed by the spirit of God only to those who are able to receive them. These secret truths Paul passes on in words that the Spirit gives him, not in "set phrases of human philosophy." Paul's claim to have the mind of Christ comes out of his belief that he receives these secret truths by revelation. Paul would like to be able to teach the Corinthians this esoteric divine wisdom, but they are not yet *pneumatikoi*,[22] and the real wisdom is reserved for the *teleioi*. Reitzenstein points out, as noted in another connection, that there are three classes of people in Gnosticism: *sarkikoi* (equivalent to *sarkinoi* of I Cor. 3:1), *psuchikoi* (I Cor. 2:14), and *pneumatikoi* (I Cor. 3:1); the mysteries also have three classes, unbelievers, proselytes *(religiosi)*, and *teleioi*, the fully initiated.

Gnostic and mystery terminologies are even more marked in Colossians. Indeed the Pauline authorship of Colossians has been doubted on the ground of its speculative elements. This does not seem necessary if we grant the opportunistic character of Paul's teaching and his supreme conviction of the sufficiency of Christ to meet all

[22] Reitzenstein defines a *pneumatiker* as a person who has *gnosis* added to *pneuma*.

human needs. He has shown himself at home in the mystery cult terminology. He would naturally be acquainted with the religious approach of the Gnostics.[23] Cosmological speculation had penetrated the Graeco-Roman world, propagated by the mysteries. All three elements are present in the letter. The position of Christ is the great secret of the ages (1:26), which has been disclosed to the Christians, who according to God's will are to make this secret known to every man and present him *teleios*. This is an individualistic approach. In Christ's reconciling function man has been forgiven because the Cross in its cosmic significance has satisfied God (3:13). Paul craves a fuller *gnosis* of God for the Christians (1:9), the benefit that comes from "knowing Christ" (2:2), that divine mystery in which all treasures of "wisdom" and "knowledge" are found (2:3). This seems to be a direct response to their situation. It is a religious quest that they are engaged in. This is the same Christ with whom the Christian was *buried* in baptism, the rite that renders circumcision so superfluous. The Christian is stripped of his material nature, raised to life with Christ by the very power of God (2:12). This being the case, the old man is dead, the Christian's life is hidden with Christ in God (3:3, the kind of absorption they ought to crave), and will be present in glorified form with him at the *Parousia* (3:4). This has important bearing upon conduct.

The same spiritistic elements that we find elsewhere in Paul are present here. Their faith is "in Christ" (1:4), their love toward each other was awakened by the Spirit (1:8). Paul prays God to fill them with the knowledge of God's will through "full spiritual wisdom and insight"

[23] J. Carlyon, "Paul and the Gnostic Quest" (unpublished dissertation, University of Chicago Libraries, 1926), lists twenty-five terms common to Paul and to Gnosticism.

(*en pase sophia kai sunesi pneumatike* 1:9). The mystery among the Gentiles is "Christ in you" (1:27). The goal of Christian preaching is to present every man *teleion en Christō* (1:28), which Paul works for and in which he is so mightily endued with power from God (. . . *agonizomenos kata ten energian autou ten energoumenein en emoi en dunamei* 1:29). "If you have been raised to life with Christ . . ." is spiritistic (3:1-4). Here we have the usual blend of union with Christ with the hope of the *Parousia*.

It is also in this letter that one feels the weight of that fatalism engendered by the astrological approach which has been noted in connection with Posidonius. People were weighed down by fear of the Cosmos. He meets these Christians on their own ground when he presents Christ as the preëxistent agent of creation of things seen and unseen. Since he is Lord over all, those terrifying cosmic powers are included in his dominion. These powers are personified as great, evil personal forces, which Paul calls "elements" (*stoicheia* cf. Gal. 4:3), "principalities," "dominions," "powers." Christ has conquered these; so Christians in mystic union with him are outside their domain (1:11-17). He meets these Christians too, when he declares Christ the *plerōma* of God's fulness. This cosmic Christ is head of the church; it is his body, a part of him. His resurrection has given him this place of supremacy. The effective coupling together of the "first-born of creation" with the "first-born from among the dead" links the Christian community at Colossae to the Cosmos, parts of which they have so feared. The transfer of Christians from the realm of darkness to that of God's son (1:13) was made possible by the bloody death on the Cross. Through this great cosmic act the evil powers were disarmed (2:15). These cosmic creatures, whom they, through fear, have worshipped, have been conquered (1:18, 20).

While first-century intellectualism was eclectic, the philosophical writings of the period breathe a different spirit from that which we have just described in connection with Paul's mysticism and the syncretistic religious outlook at Colossae, which Paul attempted to meet. Here it would seem we have another extensive area of thought in which Paul does not link up with the main intellectual current of the first century. And when we turn to consider what the Stoic intellectuals of the period were concerned with, the conclusion is the same. The Stoic would probably not have been out of sympathy with Paul's powers of endurance as illustrated in II Cor. 11:23-33. He would probably have objected to his manner of recounting them. Certainly the Stoic would have scorned Paul's outbursts of emotion in the letters to the Thessalonians, to the Philippians, and in II Corinthians, chapters 1-7. There is nothing of the "philosophic calm" about Paul. Seneca's ideal for the philosopher could never be attained by Paul: "The philosopher's speech like his life should be composed; and nothing that rushes headlong is well ordered."[24] Paul had little in common with the Stoic ideal of "freedom from passion, from every disturbing emotion, desire and fear, excessive pain and pleasure, anger, so that we may enjoy that calm of soul and freedom from care which bring moral stability and dignity of character."[25]

The Stoic insistence upon being guided by reason was not the Pauline ideal. To Paul the natural man needed the divine increment of Spirit before he could function

[24] Seneca *Epistle* 40.
[25] Cicero *De Officiis* i. 20. Translated by Walter Miller, Loeb Classical Library (New York, 1921).

successfully. The Stoic was a self-made man. It was his responsibility to exercise his will, to avoid what was not in his power, to follow reason, to be mentally unperturbed.[26] Paul was altogether too much "consumed with anxiety" to have been much influenced by the intellectualism of his day with its divergent emphases. It was not Paul's confidence in man that led to his conviction that the goal of Christian preaching was to present every man *teleion en Christō*. It was rather his confidence in the power of the Spirit working in even unpromising material (I Cor. 6:9-10). There is no indication that Paul trusted the human reason to make of man what he ought to become. Nor did he share the idea that man was akin to God by virtue of his participation in the universal Reason *(Logos)*.

§4

We have seen that Paul shows no affinity with the Stoic philosophers of the period in his major affirmations as they appear in the non-paraenetic or primary sections of the letters. The sphere of ethical teaching was of particular interest to Stoics, and it appears probable that if Stoic influence were to be found anywhere in Paul's letters it would be in those sections devoted to the inculcation of ethical precepts, since, to recur to Lightfoot: "It is difficult to estimate and perhaps not very easy to overrate the extent to which Stoic philosophy had leavened the moral vocabulary of the civilized world at the time of the Christian era." We may well ask, "What Stoic influence is evident in the definitely ethical sections of Paul's letters?" It is a matter of common knowledge that moral precepts tend to rigidity of formulation in the course of time. This

---

[26] Seneca *On the Firmness of the Wise Man* and Epictetus *Discourses* i. 6. are good examples of the Stoic outlook.

WAS PAUL AN INTELLECTUAL? 127

is amply illustrated in Jewish literature in Proverbs and Eccleciasticus (Wisdom of Jesus ben Sirach). The implications of the fact of the democratic formulation of ethical precepts and of their origin in social experience are not always recognized by students of the ethical teaching of Paul. A notable exception to this is found in the work of the contributors to the *Handbuch zum Neuen Testament* in the commentaries on the letters of Paul.

Hans Lietzmann in his commentary on Romans in an excursus on 1:21 gives a convenient summary of the vice-lists in Paul's letters, as well as of the source material for the study of Stoic vice-lists. There are unmistakable evidences of such lists in Hellenistic-Jewish literature too, showing that the Stoic tendency was quite general in the literature with which Paul might be expected to be acquainted.[27] Karl Weidinger shows the same thing to be true in regard to the *haustafel* pattern for the inculcation of moral precepts pertaining to the household.

A classic passage for the study of Stoic influence on Paul is Rom. 2:14-16.

When the Gentiles who have no law naturally do the things that the Law commands, though they have no law are a law unto themselves, for they show the commands of the Law written upon their hearts, and their consciences will bear witness and afterwards their thoughts will either accuse or defend them on the day when God through Jesus Christ, as my gospel asserts, will judge the secrets of men.

A fundamental axiom of Stoic ethics is that ethical action is the result of a law of nature planted within man which has its basis in divinity. A man lives ethically when he lives "according to nature." Man has within him a spark of the divine reason; it is part of his heritage as a man.

[27] Hans Lietzmann, *An Die Römer* (Tübingen, 1928), pp. 35-36.

Hellenistic Judaism brought the Jewish Law and the Stoic law of nature into a close relationship, and taught that the Law of Moses was the complete expression of the Stoic law of nature. Jewish apologists like Philo saw no difficulty in making Moses responsible for Greek philosophy because of the closeness of their ethical ideals.

A survey of the ethical sections of the letters of Paul does not yield a great amount of data that points to a very large debt to Stoicism as far as content of teaching is concerned. The paraenetic sections of I and II Thessalonians do not appear to betray any Stoic touches. Dibelius sees in Phil. 4:4-8 close relationship to Greek popular moral philosophy. The one Pauline example of the *haustafel* is considered in another connection. The form of Rom. 12:4-15 is allied with that of the diatribe. This chapter bears marks of much use as if it had been in existence a long time in general Christian teaching. The Pauline emphasis on Spirit is present, as we should expect from his expressed purpose in writing this letter (Rom. 1:11-13). It seems clear that in any evaluation of Stoic influence on Paul the emphasis will lie outside the primary sections of the letters.

Are we to conclude then that Paul is practically unconnected with the intellectualism of his day? The answer will depend upon the limits which we set to intellectualism. That Paul was schooled in the philosophy of the first century there is no evidence. Of the fundamental Stoic postulates there are none in Paul's writing. The major emphases of his missionary work are far removed from the Roman Stoicism of his day. The Christian movement in the Graeco-Roman world began among a class of people with whom a Cicero or a Seneca would not have troubled himself in any practical way. From the

WAS PAUL AN INTELLECTUAL? 129

extant literary remains of Roman Stoicism it would seem that Paul was not an intellectual in any sense of the word. He links up closely with the religious rather than with the philosophical aspects of Hellenism.

But there is another area in which Paul did come into contact with the intellectualism of the first century. He was influenced by Hellenistic philosophy on its non-speculative side. The dependence of Paul on the Cynic-Stoic diatribe in the area of technique and method has been established. Here is a contribution of Stoicism to Paul's preaching. We are indebted to Wendland's excellent work for a good brief account of the philosophical propaganda and the diatribe. It is difficult to disabuse our minds of the modern notion about philosophy and philosophers sufficiently to realize the democratic stamp of Hellenistic philosophy which carried over into Stoicism. The Cynic school developed a kind of "mendicant order" in philosophy, of which Diogenes was an outstanding representative. The method was popular; the preaching pithy and timely; a large following came. At first literature did not reflect this movement, but later these popular figures crept into history and then into legend. The diatribe form was created by Bion of Borysthenes who lived in the early third century B.C. Wendland considers Arrian's discourses of Epictetus a revival of the old type of diatribe, which was a peculiar mixture of earnestness and chaff.

Historians of philosophy have paid little attention to the diatribe, which is of no particular importance for the advance of philosophical thought, but this makes its cultural-historical significance even greater. We have given in another connection Wendland's picture of the Cynic preacher of the early Hellenistic age. Conditions were similar in the Roman period, and the moralists and satirists paint a gloomy picture of the time, a picture certainly exaggerated. Not that ethical emphases were lacking. The Neo-Pythagoreans stressed ethics from the first century B.C. Cynicism then arose to take up the struggle against a decadent world. The Cynic preachers equipped with cudgel and wallet belong now to the picture of Roman life in the great cities. The boundary between Cynic and Stoic is often a slender one. The popular quality of Roman philosophy is also indicated by Seneca: "There can be no doubt that philosophy has suffered a loss, now that she has exposed her charms for sale. But she can still be viewed in her sanctuary if her exhibitor is a priest and not a peddler."[28] The new diatribe ramifies into every province of life from national and family loyalties to such mundane matters as dress and food. This popular philosophy exists now in the fragments of John of Stobi. Of course there were disreputable philosophers, but there were also such men as Musonius and Epictetus whose sense of mission could not be denied.[29]

It has bearing on our subject to note that the ethical tracts of Stoics, Cynics, and Neo-Pythagoreans are similar in content, choice of theme, and tendencies, differing only in tone and shade. All schools employ the diatribe for their propaganda. If Paul could use the technique of the mystery-cult, he could use the moral utterances of a street-preacher of Tarsus or of some other city with no sense of disloyalty to his new faith. With the example of Hellenistic Judaism appropriating from Greek culture without being consciously untrue to the ancient religion, early Christianity too could borrow with no sense of perfidy; and in all probability pagan ethical precepts found ready

[28] Seneca *Epistle* 52.
[29] Wendland, *op. cit.*, pp. 86-88. Cf. Epictetus *Discourses* iii. 22. for picture of the Cynic philosopher.

WAS PAUL AN INTELLECTUAL? 131

acceptance in the new movement. As Seneca remarks, "The best ideas are common property."[30]

Wendland has a valuable section on the relation of the philosophical-ethical propaganda to Christianity. The ethical reformation, which was the goal of the philosophical preaching, prepared the soil for the new preaching. Pagan preachers, like the modern salvation army, sought the street-corners. There was a wide range of distinctly ethical-religious literature before ancient literature took over this interest. The picture of Paul in Acts 17 is a natural scene, regardless of its historicity for Paul. Wendland attributes the speedy advance of Christianity and its connection with philosophy to the spiritual atmosphere created by this popular philosophical propaganda. This is more true of the second century when philosophers began to come into the church than it is in the period of Paul. There was not much in the Christian message as Paul preached it or in the Christian meetings as they developed in his churches, that would appeal to an intellectual. Paul links up closely with Hellenistic practice, but it is in the realm of religion rather than of philosophy. The ethical standards of Paul would appeal to the pagan moralists, but they would not understand his spiritistic motivation of ethics.

There is one example of the *haustafeln* (household words) in Paul's writing. It is in Colossians 3:18 ff. The problem of this particular pattern of ethical teaching has been investigated recently. These "household words" represent early Christian teaching as it became crystallized according to a particular scheme. It is possible that they furnish a clue to the understanding of the origin of early

[30] Seneca *Epistle* 12.

Christian teaching, which in turn has bearing on the cultural history of the West.

The Colossian *haustafel* has two points of contact with I Corinthians, chapter 7, the problems of marriage and slavery. In a spirit-controlled community there is no room for such crystallization of teaching. The didactic element would be at a minimum in a group dominated by the conviction that the appearance of the Lord (*Parousia*) was at hand. As the eschatological expectations died down, the need for teaching material would be felt in a way that would not be the case in the earlier period. There would be more thought of the community life as permanent. The ethical demands reached by Paul by one route were not so very different from those reached by the pagan moralists by another. It was natural for early Christian leaders to take over current moral precepts, treasure them, reformulate them to meet their needs, Christianize them. Weidinger argues back from the *haustafeln* to less rigidly formulated sections of Paul's letters and sees in them material with a different interest from that expressed in the non-paraenetic sections.

The *haustafel* pattern is abundantly attested in three areas: Hellenistic Judaism, Hellenistic popular ethics, and Hellenistic philosophy. It may be that the Jews of the Diaspora used this pattern of moral teaching in their proselyte propaganda. It could thus have entered Christianity either by way of Judaism or of Stoicism. The influence of Judaism upon Paul is always recognized; sometimes it is overrated, seldom is it seen as something upon which the Greek spirit left its impress. Yet the Judaism of the Diaspora was the Judaism of Paul. If we had no evidence of a more direct influence of Stoicism upon Paul, we might still speak of the influence of Stoicism. But

WAS PAUL AN INTELLECTUAL? 133

there is a more direct influence. We may consider as established: the use of the diatribe, which is Stoic influence in the area of technique and method; the use of certain patterns of formulated teaching; vice and virtue-catalogues and the *haustafeln*. Even if mediated through Hellenistic Judasim, so that the borrowing was unconscious, it is certainly Stoic influence.

Paul probably would not have admitted to borrowing from the philosophy of his day any more than he would have admitted to borrowing from the mystery-cults whose deities he considered demons. Yet it is clear that from the mysteries he learned much that shaped his presentation of Christian preaching. Paul, the tent-maker of Tarsus, was not hermetically sealed from current ethical thought as it entered his environment by means of the popular street-preachers. These men were not innovators. They set forth the old, the established ideas and sought to counteract the moral decadence that they felt was threatening. They were the contribution of Stoicism to popular life, the means through which pagan ethical teaching permeated to the masses. It is by no means improbable that current pagan ethical teaching went into the formulation of the Christian ethical teaching. It is clear that the ethical sections of the Pauline letters with their tendency to the stereotyped, with their general content not designed for a specific, definite situation are not to be considered original with Paul in the same sense that we see I Corinthians, chapter 13 a product of his pen. Paul approved them, he even modified them, he probably had a share in their formulation; but they do not represent ideas peculiar to or original with him.

Having said this, we may still insist that Paul cannot be rated among the intellectuals of his day. He does not move in the same intellectual atmosphere as Seneca, Plutarch, Epictetus, or Cicero. He has no very close connection, intellectually, with his Alexandrian contemporary, Philo, who links up much more closely with the Stoicism of the period. The sphere in which Stoicism touched Paul's life was in the sphere of the affairs of everyday. Perhaps the influence was almost totally indirect; yet it was none the less real. Stoicism in its most practical aspects touched Paul's life; in its more theoretical phases there seems to have been no contact. Paul was not an intellectual.[31]

[31] See the author's article "Paul, Philo, and the Intellectuals," *Journal of Biblical Literature*, Vol. LIII, Part 2 (1934) for further research on the problem of Chapter IV.

CHAPTER V

PAUL THE JEW

NO one doubts the influence of Judaism upon Paul. There is greater willingness upon the part of many Christian writers to derive elements in Christianity from Judaism than from other possible sources. This is due, in part, to the acceptance of the Old Testament as a Christian book, and the consequent conviction that Judaism was the best of all pre-Christian religions. There have been notable studies of Judaism within the last decade. There is a tendency to greater appreciation of Jewish legalism. Christian scholars see exaggeration in the gospel picture of the Pharisees and are ready to discount that picture in the light of recent dating of the gospels and the fact of hostility between Jews and Christians, which without doubt helped to set the tone of gospel tradition as it crystallized in our present records.

The complexity of Judaism has not always been recognized. It is not always observed that the Judaism of Paul was not the same as the Judaism of Jesus, that the whole problem of Judaism cannot be subsumed under the Palestinian variety.[1] The monumental work of Professor

[1] In the most recent study of Paul's ethics Professor Enslin finds Judaism the really significant factor in determining that ethic; yet his whole treatment of Judaism is based upon the work of Professor Moore, which utilized later sources. Professor Enslin does not discuss Diaspora Judaism at all, and refers to Tarsus in the most incidental manner, ignoring the excellent work of Hans Böhlig, *Die Geisteskultur von Tarsos*.

Moore is based upon sources later than the time of Paul. The assurance that Judaism in the second century A.D. was very similar in theology and ethics is based upon the essential agreement of the Tannaite literature in these respects with the teaching of Sirach of the second century B.C.[2] Probably, but it should not be overlooked that Ecclesiasticus is a Palestinian product, that the Tannaite sources are Palestinian, and that there is evidence that Diaspora Judaism was Judaism "with a difference."

§ 1

There is abundant evidence that Judaism was not impervious to its environment. The tendency to a strict legalism set in with the reforms of Nehemiah in the fifth century B.C. This was even more acute in the Maccabean period, when the necessity of resisting Hellenization was the pressing question, and the rise of the Pharisees into prominence in the time of Herod I was but a step further in the same direction. We may generalize and say that Palestinian Judaism, because of the peculiar political circumstances of different periods, did resist change and the encroachment of Hellenism more than Diaspora Judaism was able to or found it necessary to do.

We have interesting evidence from the Elephantine papyri on Egyptian Judaism contemporary with Nehemiah. There was no such particularism in the Egyptian colony as Nehemiah and Ezra sought to bring about in Palestine. We may grant the comparative success of the leaders of Jewish legalism in Palestine, but that will not carry with it the assumption that legalistic Judaism was equally stringent in the Diaspora. One needs only to recall the works of Philo to see that Alexandrian Judaism, at least

[2] G. F. Moore, *Judaism* (Cambridge, 1927), I, 44.

PAUL THE JEW 137

in the circles of the learned, owes much to Greek philosophy. The writings of Philo, when compared with those of Paul, leave no doubt as to which of these two eminent first-century Jews came into closer touch with Gentile intellectualism. The ethical teachings of Philo, when culled from the mass of other material, bear close resemblance to Stoic ethical teaching, which as we have seen was not the case with Paul to any similar degree. Philo apparently did not have any lasting influence on Judaism. It is equally improbable that the rabbinic school in Palestine exerted any binding influence on the Alexandrian school. Palestinian Judaism was not under the same necessity of accommodating itself to Greek thought, but Philo's writings indicate the attempt to appropriate the wisdom of Greece and adapt it to what was most valued in the Jewish system.

This is not to discount the loyalty of Diaspora Jews to their ancestral faith. Philo describes the Sabbath among Greek-speaking Jews in these words:

Innumerable schools of practical wisdom and self-control and manliness and uprightness and the other virtues are opened every seventh day in all cities. In these schools the people sit decorously, keeping silence and listening with the utmost attention out of a thirst for refreshing discourse while one of the best qualified stands up and instructs them in what is best and most conducive to welfare, things by which their whole life may be made better.[3]

Paul's description in Philippians 3:5 ff. bears similar testimony. His willingness to persecute the new movement shows something of the quality of his loyalty to the religion of his fathers. And yet the indubitable fact of appropriation of language and of much of the civilization of their surroundings must not be minimized in any attempt

[3] Philo, cited by Moore, *op. cit.*, I, 306.

138   THE ETHICS OF PAUL

to understand the Jews' loyalty to Judaism. They were part of the commercial life of their day; they welcomed Gentiles in their synagogues; they were in the main stream of contemporary life.

It is necessary, too, to guard against assuming that Diaspora Judaism was similar everywhere. A knowledge of the Judaism of Alexandria will not be a guarantee for that of Tarsus. A protest that needs to be made is against setting up any norm and defining the Judaism of Paul by referring to it. Environmental factors are sufficiently diverse to account for diversity of emphasis in the same general religious pattern. There has been one study of the spiritual culture of Tarsus which is at least a recognition that only as we know Tarsus can we know Paul.[4] Böhlig draws freely upon the writings of Dio Chrysostom, who was native to this section, and who wrote about it and who was the only one to write two discourses particularly about Tarsus. He was a good observer of conditions in Asia Minor and was a younger contemporary of Paul. Böhlig further notes the tendency to derive Paul solely from Judaism and very pertinently raises the question, "What was Diaspora Judaism?"

The study of the religious and cultural history of Tarsus is complicated by the outstanding fact of syncretism. Böhlig draws freely upon the writings of Dio Chrysostom, Asia Minor to Crete and even extending to Italy. There were two ancient groups in Cilicia, the invaders and the indigenous. The former were the forerunners of the Indo-Germans, possibly to be identified with the Hittites who ruled the greater part of Asia Minor, Syria, and Palestine

[4] Hans Böhlig, *Die Geisteskultur von Tarsos* (Göttingen, 1913). We are indebted also to the archaeological researches of Sir William Ramsay for our knowledge of Tarsus. Cf. Ramsay, *The Cities of St. Paul* (New York, 1908), pp. 85-244. For the Jews of Tarsus see pp. 169-86.

PAUL THE JEW 139

from the second millennium B.C. to the rise of Tiglath Pileser of Assyria (1104 B.C.). Boundaries changed again in the seventh century and again in the Persian period. Until the time of Alexander the Great, Tarsus was a purely oriental city. In the second century B.C. a Hellenistic city arose on this oriental base. Syncretism arose less from Greek penetration eastward than from oriental penetration westward. Wave after wave of migration swept over Tarsus.

In this meeting place of East and West a colony of Jews was settled by Antiochus IV in 171 B.C., the date of the refounding of the city. Josephus states that Seleucus I granted citizenship to the Jews of such newly founded cities.[5] If this is historical, Antiochus probably followed the precedent set by Seleucus. There is the probability, therefore, that the Jews were on equal terms with Greeks. It is interesting to note that this Antiochus IV was the same Antiochus whose attempts at forcible Hellenization of Palestinian Jews precipitated the Maccabean revolt and helped to determine the mold into which Palestinian Judaism was to be cast. In the Diaspora where Hellenism was the undoubted conqueror, such a condition could not arise. The Jews were happy to be considered a special race. They coöperated with the government and lived peaceably with it. The necessity of the situation in which they were forced to a compromise justified their opinion and appeased their conscience. The inner driving motive was the utilitarian principle.

It is highly probable that Jews possessed city citizenship in the Augustan age with the privilege of firm adherence to their own religion and customs. Dio Chrysostom in a discussion of the linen weavers of Tarsus points to a

[5] Josephus *Antiquities* xii. 3. 1. Translated by W. Whiston (Boston, 1829).

development in their status in the city. At first they were not treated as the equal of the Greeks; then they were regarded as citizens; and finally they were despised as foreigners although they were born Tarsians. This seems to point to the rights of citizenship for sons by virtue of their fathers' domiciliation and links up with membership in a tribe *(phule)*, which plays a great rôle in oriental cities. This so greatly increased the number of citizens that measures were taken to curb the too rapid growth, and the rule was made that citizenship was dependent upon the payment of five hundred drachmae. This practically shut out the poor from what had been an ancient right. Dio does not mention any national, religious, or racial difference. Presumably the Jews were on the same basis.

The Jews had their own section of the city in Tarsus as in other cities. Epiphanius describes the synagogue of Tarsus as a religious and civic center. This combination is ancient. The anti-Semitism on the part of Greeks is due to the fact that the Jews were equal in many places to Greeks and Romans without taking upon themselves the tolerance due the religious customs of others. The "chosen people" idea did not fit in the Greek world.

Böhlig does not identify Diaspora Judaism with Palestinian. He is fully conscious of what alien influence would do to modify any religion. He orients Paul into the Judaism of *Tarsus*. Paul's speech shows how far the language of Diaspora Judaism was removed from that of Palestine. A Gamaliel, a Hillel, or a Shammai would not use Paul's figures of the circus, the theater, or the games. Nor did Paul's world-view arise out of Palestinian Judaism, which was influenced cosmologically by Babylonia. Here Böhlig departs from the conventional interpretation. Paul's world-view is neither Semitic nor specifically Jew-

PAUL THE JEW 141

ish. The numbers seven and twelve are Semitic, three and nine are Aryan. The latter predominate in Paul. In the Jewish consciousness of Jesus' time the horizontal world-view prevailed, whereas Paul thought in vertical terms of three worlds and three heavenly spheres. He is nearer to the apocryphal and pseudepigraphical writings than to other Jewish writings. That world-view Paul did not get from Palestinian Judaism. It became mixed with elements of Jewish belief in the Diaspora. Tarsus was the place of union where this Greek and Jewish ideology flowed together. Not only was this the Stoic, it was also the popular world-view. Third Ezra was popular among the Jews of the first century A.D. It shows how Judaism was drawn into the stream of syncretism, which had been going on since the merging of the cult of Yahweh and the cult of Baal in preëxilic times.

According to Böhlig, the point at which Tarsian Judaism stood closest to Palestinian was the place of the Law. He affirms that Diaspora Judaism believed the moral law to be more important than the ceremonial. He sees Paul as Jewish in terminology and in line of argument, but not in the whole view. The difference arises in the idea of the relation of grace to law. Judaism united the two; Paul separated them. His idea of the Law as a necessary evil, as a pedagogue, was prepared for in the Judaism of Tarsus.

In the last analysis we are thrown back upon the letters of Paul for our estimate both of the quality of his Judaism and of his estimate of it. The picture is not consistent. The letter to the Romans stands in the way of certain conclusions which could quite easily be drawn from the other letters out of the more vital situations which they portray. The letter to the Romans is the letter most often used in the attempted determination of Pauline positions. This is in line with the usual mode of approach which analyzes his *ideas* instead of his *behavior*. The present writer seeks to bring Pauline *actions* abreast of Pauline *ideas*. Both have to be considered; the problem is where to lay the emphasis.

§2

In making a survey of the letters of Paul in the effort to evaluate the Jewish elements certain things stand out. There is abundant evidence of un-Jewish behavior. There is a large element of Jewish content in his intellectual formulations. His theology contains an ever-present Jewish element. When Paul speaks of God, it is the God of the Jews that he means. All through his letters runs the idea of the supremacy of God. The term which he uses most often is "God our Father," which is a Jewish designation. Justice and mercy were the two main attributes of God in Jewish thinking. While Jesus is, for Paul, the Lord of the cult, he never displaces God. It is God who has raised him to his present high position. Paul was not conscious of any lack of monotheism, however difficult it would be for a Jew to see him as an unqualified monotheist.

Paul's cosmology, according to Böhlig, is not specifically Jewish, although this is an area in which Paul has usually been considered as leaning heavily on Jewish thought and imagery. Paul posits the heavens, the earth, and the underworld in his idea of the universe. The resurrection of Jesus from among the dead is Jewish. The idea of the resurrection of the body was a cardinal doctrine of the Pharisees, the Jewish group to which Paul belonged. The idea of the *Parousia* of Jesus in connec-

PAUL THE JEW 143

tion with the Judgment Day is Jewish. There is mention of the *Parousia* in every letter: the events detailed in I Thess. 4:16-5:9, in II Thess. 2:1-12, and in I Cor. 15:51-58. Reference to the Day of the Lord Jesus Christ is a recurring phenomenon in Paul's letters. The imagery here is definitely Jewish; perhaps the imagery of the *Parousia* of the Emperor or the similar theology of Mithraism would make the idea more intelligible to Gentile Christians than we would think possible.

There is also Paul's constant appeal to Scripture, which might be of more value as a datum on his Jewishness if he were not using the Scripture in the fashion of Philo; although, compared with Philo, he is sparing in his use of allegory, a Greek method that Philo borrowed from Greek philosophy, Stoicism in particular. Paul's appeal to the Jewish Scriptures is a constant phenomenon. Apparently he had no doubt of the orthodoxy of his position, scripturally guaranteed, just as Philo felt himself a Jew. Judged objectively, neither could qualify according to normative Judaism. Paul's use of the Scripture is that of the Hellenistic Jew.

In Galatians Paul uses the Scripture to prove a most un-Jewish position, i.e., that man's acquittal by God in the judgment is by *faith*, not by Law. By appeal to Abraham's acquittal and by allegorizing the story of Sarah and Hagar, he settles the matter to his own satisfaction. This letter stands as the most convincing evidence of Paul's un-Jewish behavior and his rationalization of it. Here are his most patent statements of the uselessness of the Law and of circumcision (5:2-4), and here also is the autobiographical section bearing witness that Paul practised what he preached (Gal. 2:1-14). Titus is held up as a fine example of Gentile Christian, who did not need circumcision to make him acceptable, and here also Paul tells of the un-Jewish behavior of himself and others in the Christian community at Antioch. Table-fellowship prevailed in this great mixed church. It is in this letter that Paul can point out that circumcision will cause the Galatians to lose their hold on God's favor, and once his indignation rises to such a height that he wishes the emasculation of his enemies who were such sticklers for circumcision (5:4, 12). Certainly this letter, in spite of the appeal to Scripture (let it be noted, to prove un-Jewish positions), cannot be cited with confidence to prove Paul a Jew in outlook. The intellectual content of resurrection, *Parousia*, appeal to Scripture, confidence in God the Father, is quite overbalanced by Paul's thoroughly un-Jewish conduct.

In the Corinthian correspondence which furnishes the most data on Paul's religious behavior, there is less Jewish emphasis although the ideas of *Parousia* and resurrection are present, and the latter is given very detailed treatment. Paul uses two Jewish figures in I Cor. 5:6-8, leaven and the Passover lamb, but in general the emphasis in these letters is preponderantly Gentile. Even the enemies are not Jews. These letters are the *locus classicus* for the description of Gentile Christianity as it functioned in a local community.

In I Thess. 2:15-16 we find anti-Jewish polemic, in Phil. 1:28-30 (probably) and 3:2-9 (certainly) we have anti-Jewish feeling expressed. In the Thessalonian passage Paul states that the preaching in Judea had been attended by persecution at the hands of the Jews. His words also indicate that he accepted the tradition that the Jews were responsible for the death of Jesus (I Thess. 2:15), and he indulges in a further bit of anti-Jewish

PAUL THE JEW 145

polemic to the effect that they are displeasing to God, hostile to mankind, and are ever on the alert to keep Christian missionaries from working with Gentiles. It may be that Paul is expanding and adapting polemic already current in Christian circles.

The second passage in Philippians is the most extreme that we find in Paul. After a hateful reference to circumcision as mutilation he goes on to the assertion that the Christians are the true circumcision, just as he had once called them the "true Israel of God" (Gal. 6:16). They are the real adherents of Judaism, who worship God in the right fashion. They take pride only in Christ and do not rely on any external or physical means (Phil. 3:3-4). Paul then lists the things in which as a Jew he had taken pride, only to have them serve as an introduction to the picture he draws of his new status in Christ. In comparison with his present advantages, the former advantages seem nothing but refuse. In his heightened state of feeling Paul uses the strongest term he can find *(skubalon)*. Here is a thoroughgoing repudiation of all that he had once held sacred. In this passage he says that no fault could be found with his Judaism formerly, that by the standard of the Law he was blameless (Phil. 3:6). He had also told the Galatians of his former devotion to the Law and to the traditions of his forefathers (Gal. 1:14).[6]

These two passages (Gal. 1:13-14; Phil. 3:5-9), brief though they are, are definite evidence of the type of Jewish home in which Paul was reared. We may never guarantee that Pharisaism was the same everywhere, or that it

[6] Paul's statement "by the Law's standard of righteousness no fault could be found with me" (Phil. 3:6) does not fit with what Paul says of his life under the Law in Romans 7:9-11, if that chapter is to be taken as biographical data. The passage in Romans is followed by a statement of the Christian's new status (Rom. 8) just as in Philippians Paul's outburst against Judaism's advantages is followed by a description of his new status (Phil. 3:7 ff.).

was a unity in thought and conduct, but from the few verses in Paul about the Judaism of his former days we know that the general Pharisaic pattern of religious behavior held in his Tarsus home. The things to which as a Jew he could point with pride were: circumcision on the eighth day, membership in the tribe of Benjamin, the Pharisaic attitude toward the Law, and the traditions of the elders. We have Josephus' witness that the Pharisees were highly respected by the Jewish people as a whole.

It is probable that Paul's family was more strict in its observance of the Pharisaic custom than were the rank and file of Diaspora Jews, although the fact that Paul's Old Testament was the Septuagint shows how far even this orthodox family had travelled in the direction of the assimilation of Greek ideas. They doubtless observed all the important festivals and fast-days and other ceremonies which belong in the religious pattern of Pharisaic Judaism. As Diaspora Jews they were relieved of the duties pertaining to the Temple cultus, finding in the synagogue their religious center. Paul would attend the synagogue school, would be taught the traditions of his race, and at the proper time would become a "son of the Law" with the responsibility to keep the Torah. It was distinctly a group religion that Paul was born into. The Jew was no individualist except in the responsibility to observe the Torah, and even at this point group customs and group sanctions contributed much to the religious life in a normal Jewish home.

Paul's few statements about the Judaism of his past make it clear that his family accepted the standard of the Torah and endeavored to live up to its demands. Paul declares himself an enthusiastic adherent of the tradition; in fact he believes that he outstripped most of his young

Tarsian contemporaries in his devotion to the Law and the tradition (Gal. 1:14). The fact that Paul nowhere mentions his tutelage under Gamaliel, even when he is reviewing his advantages as a Jew or defending his apostleship before a hostile group of Corinthian Christians, should give us pause before a too ready acceptance of that tradition in Acts. Paul would hardly have omitted such an important item as this tradition had it been founded upon fact.[7]

Whether we accept this tradition or not, there is no doubt about Paul's fanatical devotion to his ancestral religion. His devotion went beyond the bounds of a normal healthy-minded attitude towards his religious and racial traditions. He was willing to persecute those who differed from himself. Most Jews felt no urge to coerce their fellow-Jews who had made a transfer of loyalties and were seeing in Christianity something that satisfied them. Paul could never do things by halves. That same inability to see himself in the wrong, which is revealed so clearly in the situations of conflict in which we have found him, was present in his pre-conversion days as in his life as a Christian missionary.

Paul gives very little information about the experience which changed his religious direction, that experience which he interprets as divinely mediated. It resulted in a transfer of loyalties. All the devotion that had gone into the old religion now went into the new. Conversion was not a normal experience in Judaism. The Jew was born into his tradition; it was carefully taught him; he took satisfaction in his racial and religious status. He was shown what to do to be acceptable to God, and he very

[7] M. S. Enslin, "Paul and Gamaliel," *Journal of Religion*, VII (1927), pp. 360-75.

definitely had to work out his own salvation. His wrongdoing was atoned for by his repentance, but here too, *he* played the chief rôle in the process of reëstablishing his status with God. The Torah was given him to be kept; he did not despair of his ability to do so or grow morbid over his failures.

Assuming that Paul was a normal Jew with a normal religious experience within Judaism, it is very difficult to account for his conversion to a very different type of religion. The fact that Paul went through such a right-about-face experience shows that he was not deriving the usual satisfactions from his ancestral religion. The position that Rom. 7:7-25 is an account of Paul's preconversion struggle has not yet been successfully overthrown by any of the rival theories of scholars. The indubitable evidence that Paul willingly persecuted the Hellenistic Christian group shows that he was abnormal. Psychologists classify this tendency to cruelty as sadism.

Paul's temperament as a Christian is capable of abundant illustration from his own writings. There is considerable evidence that points to emotional instability, strong individualism which insists upon dominating, abnormal capacity for hardships, and readiness for martyrdom. These factors point to a high degree of probability that Paul was temperamentally unsuited for a satisfying religious experience within Judaism and that his emotional temperament did not thrive on the practices of an "attainment religion" with emphasis on the group instead of upon the individual. That Paul was temperamentally unfitted for a satisfying religious experience in Judaism is no fair criterion, of course, by which to judge its efficacy for other Jews. Paul admits that he found only two Jews among his converts that were a comfort to him in his work for the

PAUL THE JEW 149

kingdom of God (Col. 4:11). On the other hand, the presence of Jewish content in his intellectual formulations is quite natural out of his background, but it must not be allowed to obscure the more important fact that Paul behaved in very un-Jewish fashion and justified his conduct. If we take Galatians, Thessalonians, Philippians and the Corinthian letters there is no doubt where the emphasis lies. Paul was predominantly un-Jewish in conduct, and he definitely discounts Judaism too, in spite of the ever-present element of Jewish ideology in his intellectual formulations.

But one of the major productions of Paul stands in the way of this sweeping conclusion, i.e., the letter to the Romans. Here Paul speaks very appreciatively of the Law: "the Law itself is holy, and each command is holy, just and good" (Rom. 7:12). His attitude toward Jews, too, is much more appreciative than that of Philippians 3:2-9. He devotes a section (Rom. 9-11) to proving that God has not cast off the Jews, that the rejection of Christ by the present generation of Jews does not mean their repudiation as a race. The fact that Romans does not fit into the Pauline picture depicted by the other letters in respect to his attitude towards Jews and Judaism necessitates a careful examination of this letter.

§3

It is particularly difficult to write with any confidence about the circumstances of the letter to the Romans. Critical questions are raised that belong to the province of New Testament introduction, and yet it is necessary to have a working hypothesis on such matters before it is possible to determine its relative value in comparison with the letters of Paul to his own churches. This letter does not paint a picture such as we find in the other genuine letters of Paul, particularly those which arise out of the heat of controversy, as Galatians, or those which find Paul on the defensive, as Corinthians. Yet it is this letter that is emphasized and the other letters that are discounted, in cases where the picture as a whole is not consistent. It seems to the present writer that it is a debatable question as to which letters ought to be discounted. May it not be probable that in the more living vital situations of the groups which he knew personally, we have the real Paul? This letter is Pauline, but it is Paul in a mood in which we do not usually find him. This letter is carefully constructed even to the point of artificiality. It is more conciliatory with reference to the Jews and to the Law than any other letter in which Paul mentions these matters. How did such letter happen to be written?[8]

It seems evident that there is no pressing, vital issue such as we find in Galatians and in Corinthians. Paul's expressed purpose in visiting them is to "impart some spiritual gift," and in Chapter 15 he outlines certain plans that he has for the future (15:22-33). Evidently the Christianity of the church at Rome was non-spiritistic, which to Paul would seem defective in spite of his appreciation of them (1:8; 15:14). He wants to have his labors bear fruit among them as among the rest of the Gentiles (1:11-13). He is ambitious to preach in Rome (1:15). Certain things are clear from Chapter 15. Paul is about to set out for Jerusalem with the collection that the Christians of Greece and Macedonia had contributed to the

---

[8] Certain difficult questions attach to this letter. There is doubt about Chapters 15-16, since this letter early existed in two forms, with and without these chapters. Certain early copies also omitted "in Rome." Was it first a general letter to mixed churches that he had not visited, to which Chapters 15-16 were later added as a covering letter for Rome? See K. Lake, *The Earlier Epistles of Paul* (London, 1911), p. 362.

Christian churches of Judea (15:25). He hopes that he may escape the Jews in Judea and that he will be favorably received by the Christians there (15:31). This mission safely over, he plans to go to Spain, at which time he will stop in Rome for a visit (15:24).

To those who adopt the hypothesis of an Ephesian imprisonment as the place from which the letters of the imprisonment proceeded, Romans becomes the last letter Paul wrote. If Professor Ropes is correct in his assumption that the Judaistic controversy was settled early and that Romans therefore is not to be explained as dealing primarily with the same issue, the contention of Professor Lütgert that Gentile Christians are being warned not to disregard the Law gains in probability. To see chapters 9-11 as designed to exhort Gentile Christians with antinomian tendencies, to respect the ethical standards of the Law is not fanciful when we recall the trouble that Paul had in Corinth with this very matter. The circumstances surrounding the writing to the Romans then become something like this: Paul, about to set out on a long and dangerous journey, hopes to find Roman support for his future mission to Spain; Paul recently through a hard fight in Corinth—mainly settled in his favor, but enmity still in existence—Paul seeing the Roman church not appreciating sufficiently the Pauline type of Christianity with its emphasis on Spirit, at the same time apprehensive lest the movement turn more and more antinomian, decides to leave a document setting forth in calm and conciliatory fashion the main points on which Christians find it difficult to agree. The document at the same time will contain a careful exposition of the peculiarly Pauline positions.

The letter bears the marks of careful construction. It falls into four well-defined sections: chapters 1-5; 6-8;

9-11; 12-15.[9] After an unusually long and stately introduction (1:1-17) Paul develops at some length the theme that the whole human race is unrighteous (1:18-3:20). The picture of the Gentile world in 1:18-32 has become the classic description of Gentile wickedness. It represents the taking over of traditional material. It reflects the Wisdom of Solomon, chapters 12-14, and is the Jewish view of the Gentile world. The vice-lists were a common device of Stoicism and of Hellenistic Judaism. Yet it is true that "he was not dependent on any literary description of Gentile wickedness for his knowledge of Gentile character. He had been brought up in a great Gentile city and was writing in one notorious for its immorality."[10]

Paul turns to the Jew, and his picture of Jewish unrighteousness is just as scathing as that of the Gentile. Particularly does he castigate the Jew for his feeling of moral superiority over the Gentile (2:1-4, 17-23). Repentance is what the Jew needs. The possession of the Jewish Law is no guarantee of righteousness as they suppose (2:12-16), for righteousness is a matter of the heart and not of race (2:25-29). God shows no partiality. Thus far Paul's argument deflates both Gentile and Jew on the score of morals. Jew and Gentile are on a level.

In the light of all this Paul might well ask if the Jews have no advantage (3:1-2). If he came in touch with many Jews he was probably asked this question, too. The Jew could not give up his prerogatives easily. Was he not of God's chosen race, to whom God's promise had been made in the dim far away past? Paul himself, when faced with the implications of his own individualism, might well shrink from the logic of his own position.

[9] E. I. Bosworth, *Romans* (New York, 1919), pp. 76-81, gives a brief but clear analysis of the letter.
[10] *Ibid.*, p. 102.

After all, privilege is dear, and if there is anything to this matter of being a Jew why not profit by it? Paul here seems to think that there was an advantage in spite of his having called it "refuse" on another occasion. The argument of the Jews, that it would not be fair for God to inflict punishment upon them because their unrighteousness serves to bring into clearer relief the righteousness of God, is scorned by Paul. As well say, "Let us do evil that good may come of it." The whole idea is absurd (3:5-8). On the other hand, the Jews are not at a disadvantage, for he has just made clear that the whole world is under the control of sin (3:9), which Paul proves by the selection of appropriate proof-texts, leading up to the thoroughly Pauline position, "For no human being can be pronounced acquitted in the sight of God by doing what the Law commands" (3:20). This is exactly the position of Gal. 2:16. All that the Law can do is to make men conscious of sin (3:20).

These vivid pictures of Gentile and Jewish unrighteousness are thrown upon Paul's screen to provide a background for his statement of acquittal through faith in Jesus Christ (3:21-31). The usual Pauline theology is clear here. God's method of declaring men acquitted is an anciently attested one. The Scriptures bear witness to it, and Paul launches into a long discussion of the relative antiquity of this method in comparison with the method of Law. Abraham was acquitted by faith long before he was circumcised (4:10-11). David, too, is an ancient witness to acquittal through faith, apart from actions (4:6-8). Christ has an important rôle in the acquittal process. The term "sacrifice of reconciliation" (3:25) savors of Col. 2:14 where the Cross of Christ is exhibited. The death of Christ is an evidence of the love of God for sinners. It is a reconciliation process: man becomes reconciled, shares the life of Christ, finds peace with God (5:6-11). This contributes directly to man's life: "more than that let us glory in our troubles, for we know that trouble brings about endurance, and endurance approval, and approval hope, and hope will not put us to shame" (5:3-4).

Paul's mode of argumentation comes out clearly in 5:12-21. One man, Adam, introduced sin, and consequently death, into the world; this sentence was for a condemnation that all men share. Through one man, Jesus Christ, came the mercy of God into the world, which results in acquittal for all men. Man seems to have sinned through Adam as well as individually. Adam's disobedience had disastrous results; Christ's obedience gives to the mass of men acquittal. The Law multiplied men's sins, but God's mercy through Christ surpassed men's sins (5:18-21).

At the end of Paul's first carefully thought-out argument one sees no very definite bearing on any conceivable situation at Rome. Romans is a product of the study, quite apart from any definite vital situation. One feels the building up of an argument for the sake of the un-Jewish message of Paul, acquittal through faith. There is no particular brief for Judaism in this section. Its purpose is to provide a background for the next great question he will discuss, the relation of the acquitted man to sin. Paul met criticism at this point. Jews could point to the antinomianism of certain Christians. Paul knew by experience in Corinth that their criticism was justified. Gentiles made assumptions on the basis that "by the Law can no one be pronounced acquitted." Chapters 6-8 show how Paul met this Jewish criticism and the Gentiles' unwarranted assumptions. Paul argues for the ethical basis of his position. "Are we to remain in sin, that grace may increase? God forbid! We who have died to sin, how can we live in it still" (6:1)? This argument is based upon the fact of the Christian's union with Christ through the burial in baptism (6:3-5). The old self is actually crucified with Christ. Christ has been raised from the dead. "Think thus about yourselves, as dead to sin, but alive to God since you are in Christ" (6:11). "Sin must no longer rule you, for you are living not under Law but under grace" (6:14). If the church at Rome was a non-spiritistic church, they must have had a hard time understanding Paul at this point. The terminology is similar to that of the mysteries, however, which would have helped.

Every person is in a state of slavery to something. The Christian has exchanged masters. He is now a slave to God, through his union with Christ (6:22-23), which guarantees him eternal life, that common promise of the mystery cults. Their situation is analogous to that of the woman whose husband died thus loosing her from the marriage law (7:1-3). The Christian after he joins the body of Christ is dead to the Law (7:4). In his new state the dominance of sin should be an impossibility.

The natural interpretation of 7:7 ff. is to treat it as a bit of spiritual autobiography, although this is sometimes disputed. Paul has made a statement in 7:5 that the Law awoke the sinful passions, which operating through the members of the body bore fruit unto death. This would give point to the contention that the Law was sin, something which Paul wants to avoid. He insists that the Law is not sin, but sin's revealer. He would never have known sin but for the Law. He uses the specific illustration of the command against covetousness (7:7-8).

Apart from the Law sin is dead. I was apart from the Law once. When the command came, sin revived, and I died. And I found the command which was intended for life to be death. And sin taking the opportunity through the command deceived me, and through it I died. So the Law is holy, and each command is holy, just and good (7:9-12).

The Law came in in order to increase the offense. But where sin increased, favor increased much more. So that as sin ruled by death favor might rule through righteousness unto eternal life through Jesus Christ our Lord (5:20-21).

The first passage is contradictory. A holy Law, with each command holy, just, and good, was the agency that gave sin an opening to carry on its deceitful work. Paul further points out that in his own case when the command came "sin awoke and I died." He hastens to relieve the Law of responsibility for this "death," by personifying "sin" as an evil force in his life. This is in line with Paul's dualism, which posits man as under control of supernatural forces wherever he turns; sin has possession of him. His only hope is to exchange masters: Christ in exchange for sin.

The picture Paul presents in 7:14-25 is one of struggle between the higher and the lower elements of man's nature. In contemporary Judaism it was thought that evil action of men was caused by the "evil impulse" implicit in man from birth, but the connection of this evil inclination with the body or flesh *(sarks)* is in line with Hellenistic thought. It is the natural outcome of the changes which overtook Greek philosophy in the Hellenistic period. It is present in Posidonius and in Philo, and also in the mysticism of the Hermetic writings.[11] Paul is vivid in portrayal:

---

[11] Hans Lietzmann, *An Die Römer* (Tübingen, 1928), excursus on "Das Fleisch und die Sünde," pp. 75-77.

PAUL THE JEW 157

For we know that the Law is spiritual, but I am of the flesh, sold to sin as a master. I do what I do not understand. I do what I do not want to do. I do what I hate. . . . It is no longer I that do these things, it is sin which dwells in me. For I know that nothing good lives in my flesh. To wish to do right is present in me, but I do not accomplish it; I do not do the good which I want to do, but the bad which I do not want to do. But if I do what I do not want to do, it is not I that do it, but sin that lives in me. But I find another law in my body in struggling with the law of my mind, which makes me a prisoner to the law of sin in my body (7:14-23).

If this is in any measure autobiographical, even though modified in the light of his experience as a Christian, it would seem to indicate that Paul as a Jew found it truly impossible to realize the standard of the Torah, in the sense that the Christian finds the command "Be ye perfect as your heavenly father is perfect" unrealizable. Of an intensely emotional temperament his inability to realize the standards of the Torah worried him, as psychologists often find to be the case with emotionally unstable Christians. Paul was not a normal Jew. The normal Jew was satisfied with an approximation to an unrealizable ideal. In the light of the above passage it is understandable that Paul was temperamentally unsuited for a religion like Judaism. He belongs to the condition described by Gilbert Murray as a "failure of nerve." "Miserable man that I am! Who will rescue me from this doomed body? Thank God! it is through Christ our Lord" (7:25).

That bit of autobiography prepares for the enthusiastic exposition of Paul's central tenet, "life in Christ." Christ did for man what the Law could not do, namely, enabled the Christian to achieve in his own experience the ethical standard of the Law. Christ performs a double function: union with him makes the Christian powerful over sin, and the death of Christ was an act of God by which certain obligations were cancelled. The death was necessary to get Christ into the place where he could be of help to man in reënforcing his nature with the new increment of "spirit" which is the normal possession of the Christian.

Those who are of the flesh only are not able to please God. But you are not of the flesh, but of the spirit, if the Spirit of God dwells in you. If any man does not have Christ's Spirit he is not his. . . . If the Spirit of him who raised Jesus from among the dead lives in you, he who raised Christ Jesus from among the dead will make your bodies to live by means of his Spirit which lives in you (8:9, 11).

Possession of the Spirit is the only way to avoid death. All who are guided by God's Spirit are God's sons (8:14). Paul clearly conditions ethical achievement in human experience by the person's possession of this supernatural power in his life. The figure of adoption which Paul uses here does not lead to any cheap and easy relationship for the Christian, "Heirs of God and fellow-heirs with Christ, if we share his sufferings in order to share his glory" (8:17).

Paul raises the whole matter to the cosmic plane in 8:18-25. Creation is waiting with bated breath for the great disclosure of the sons of God. The Spirit is the pledge of future redemption. Here is the theory of divine election that has so influenced later Christian theology (8:28-30). Paul is not troubled about the arbitrariness of God, for 8:31-39 is one of the most magnificent hymns of triumph in all religious literature. "If God is for us, who can be against us?" sets the tone of the great triumphal ode. Paul paints a compelling picture. God is on the side of the Christians whom he had loved well enough to make his own son the supreme gift to men.

PAUL THE JEW 159

Through this gift of God man secures acquittal by God in the great assize. Christ is in the presence of God pleading for men, and finally comes the triumphant conclusion that nothing can separate the Christian from Christ's love. Paul looks back on trouble, persecution, hunger, destitution, danger, and sword and is able to say,

For I am persuaded that neither death nor life, neither angels nor sovereignties, neither things present nor things to come, nor powers nor heights nor depths will be able to separate us from the love of God which is in Christ Jesus, our Lord (Rom. 8:38-39).

This is the highest religious peak in the letter, and judging from the catalogue of events in II Cor. 11:22-33 it is from the depths of personal experience and conviction.

It is very evident that Judaism is not the background out of which Paul argues in chapters 6-8. It is a clear setting forth of Pauline religion as it allies itself with Gentile modes of thought. It is a plea for spiritistic emphases in religion as against a more didactic religion.

Were it not for chapters 9-11 and Paul's defense of the Law in 7:12-13, Paul would convict himself out of his own statements as anti-Jewish and as utterly repudiating his ancestral faith. Particularly if Romans is Paul's last letter does it appear clear why he writes as he does, and why it is so different in attitude towards the Jews and Judaism. Paul had his major responses to the Christian message from Gentiles. By the time he is ready to set out for Jerusalem to visit the Christians there, they are quite in the majority in the Pauline churches. This has given them the feeling that they have supplanted the Jews in God's favor. Moreover, some of them were inclined to put a wrong construction on Paul's teaching about freedom from the Law, and licentiousness was the result. This would lead Paul to speak more kindly of the Jews than he might otherwise have done. The fact that Paul is able to see his theological positions in the ancient Scriptures makes him unable to see why the Jews can be so stupid or so perverse as not to see that Christianity is real Judaism. In all probability Paul believed with entire sincerity that Christianity was the religion of his forefathers carried on to fulfillment, and it caused him genuine grief to see his fellow-countrymen outside the Christian movement.

His argument is simple. He is not against his fellow-countrymen; he hopes to see them in the new movement (9:1-5), nor should the present unbelief of the Jews be interpreted that God does not mean them to be saved; God is merely exercising his prerogative of arbitrary selection as he did in the past (9:6-13) and who are the Gentiles to question what God does! To be sure they have outdone the Jews in respect to righteousness, although the Jews have tried hard, but in the wrong way, seeking acquittal through works rather than through faith (9:32). They meant well, they were devoted to God, but not with an intelligent devotion, for they ignored His way of pronouncing people acquitted. They did not realize that "Christ marks the end of the Law" so that anyone who has faith may attain acquittal (10:4).

The faith way is so plain and obvious that Jews are not to be condoned for not having accepted it and made it their own (10:6-13). The way is so simple:

For if with your lips you acknowledge that Jesus is Lord and if in your heart you believe that God raised him from among the dead, you will be saved. . . . For the Scripture says "Every one who believes on him will not be put to shame." For there is no distinction of Jew and of Greek, for all have the same Lord bounteous to all who call upon him. For everyone who calls upon the name of the Lord will be saved (10:9-10, 12-13).

Moreover, since it had been so widely preached, there is no excuse for not having heard it, but the Scriptures set forth their conduct, first by Moses and then by Isaiah (10:19-21).

Paul sets out deliberately to mitigate any undue Gentile conceit. Paul and other Jews in the movement are sufficient to show that God has not cast off his people; he has selected a small remnant for salvation. The insensibility of the majority ought not to surprise a Jew or a Gentile who knows the Scriptures; Isaiah and David pointed it out long ago. The great numbers of Gentiles will make the Jews jealous, and in time they will come in; in fact, that is why Paul had worked so hard with Gentiles. Let the Gentiles remember that they have the inferior position, that they are the wild olive grafted on to the main trunk. God is quite capable of treating them as he has the Jews (11:21). After all, it is only the present generation of Jews that are insensible to the Christian movement. After the Gentiles have been saved, the mass of the Jewish nation will come crowding in. They will experience the same favor as the Gentiles: "For God has made all men prisoners of disobedience, that he might show favor to them all. How deep are God's riches, wisdom and knowledge, how unsearchable are his judgments, how untraceable are his ways!" (11:32-33).

In this brief sketch of the non-paraenetic section of the letter to the Romans the attempt has been made to show by an inductive process Paul's attitude towards Jews and Judaism. This is the letter which shows Paul sympathetic to his race and appreciative of its ethical outlook as expressed in the Law. Yet in no letter is the insufficiency of the Law as a means of salvation more clearly shown, for nowhere do we have clearer formulation of the peculiarly Pauline emphases in religion than in chapters 6-8. Nowhere do we have such clearly built-up arguments of the basic position of guidance by the Spirit. This letter is thoroughly Pauline. The absence of controversy, except the imaginary one demanded by the diatribe style, which is used in this letter, tends to make the hypothesis that it was a circular letter, not limited to Rome, an attractive one. Paul's other letters bear the marks of conflict. This more cool dispassionate argument reads like a final document prepared to vindicate his peculiar positions, i.e., of spiritistic religion, combined with an insistence upon rigidly ethical conduct. The one emphasis is criticised by the Jews, the other by the Gentiles, who are inclined to carry Paul's position of freedom to its logical conclusion, and that conclusion was abhorrent to Paul.

§4

The paraenetic section of this letter, chapters 12-15, proves the timeliness of Weidinger's warning against the usual exegesis of such sections. There seems to be no reason why chapters 12-14 should have a special bearing on Rome, particularly chapter 12. If this chapter is Paul's, it is Paul at his best ethically. If it is general Christian teaching, early formulated, the Christians were not like the antinomian group of Corinth. The chapter bears the Pauline stamp. At the outset Paul urges the Christians to be transformed by the renewal of their minds—the familiar emphasis of Paul upon the reënforcement of the natural man by the endowment of the Spirit—all to a religio-ethical goal, that they may find out the good and pleasing and perfect will of God (12:1-2). One can see his experience back of his admonition that Christians are not to think of themselves more highly than they ought to think. Paul is writing in Corinth where some Christians were not inclined to think soberly of themselves, as his scornful sarcasm of II Corinthians, chapters 10-13 shows. He uses again one of his favorite analogies for illustrating the ideal functioning of the Christian community, the figure of the human body as symbolizing the body of Christ (12:4-8). He recognizes different degrees of faith as coming from God. This may be reference to the fact that all Christians did not show an equal amount of faith, since it savors of the treatment of the "gifts" (*charismata*) of the Corinthian community.

The section on love found in 12:9-21 needs little exposition; it is clear as it stands. This is the most important treatment of human relations that we have in the Pauline letters. What was its origin? It is only too clear that Paul, while he certainly approved this high ideal, did not practise it consistently. He did not always bless those that persecuted him; he called them "dogs," "mutilators." With this calm, tempered, high-minded setting forth of the Christian ethic, II Corinthians, chapters 10-13 has little in common. "Avenge not yourselves"; Paul proposed to avenge himself on his third visit to Corinth (II Cor. 13:1 ff.) if they did not bow to his unquestioned, God-given authority. "If it be possible, as much as lies in you [it did not lie in Paul] be at peace with all men." It seems that this does not fit Paul's temperament, but perhaps we have no right to judge a man by the times when he displays his worst side in fighting for what he prizes most. We have as little right, however, to ignore the other times when he is bitter, vulgar, and contemptuous. Perhaps here we may appeal to the hypothesis recently advanced and see in this the activity of those surviving friends of Jesus who were not interested primarily in the Messianic glorification of their leader, but who remembered the teaching and attempted to preserve it.[12] The method of *Formgeschichte* would point to the early formulation of Christian teaching.

Chapter 13 might appear to link up directly with Rome, but there is no constraining evidence that would show its reference to duty to the state, its taxes and customs, to be directed against the Romans. In the provincial cities the Christians would meet the strong arm of the Empire perhaps even more zealously administered, as was the case when Emperor worship was so much appreciated in the provinces. In one respect this chapter is difficult to link up with Paul. Here is clear idealization of the Empire from one who had suffered beatings from its officials. This is not a normal outlook from the man who reacts so differently against personal enemies. Böhlig points out that in chapter 13 the typical point of view of Diaspora Judaism is expressed. This is a persuasive argument to Christians not to stir up trouble against a powerful ruler. It is good practical advice; it would not appeal to revolutionaries of the type of Judas and Saddouk, but it shows young Christianity ready to abide by its temporal heads. It may be current teaching Christianized. Perhaps the eschatology of early Christianity had something to do with the quietistic outlook. It should be noted that Emperor worship had not yet arisen. It is in line with Paul's insistence upon the preservation of the *status quo*, as we have seen in the Corinthian situation (I Cor. 7:17 ff.).

It is even more difficult to see the particular bearing of chapter 14 on Rome. Why should a chapter dealing with diet be especially applicable in a group where Paul would be expected to be personally acquainted with individual Christians only? This is a careful exposition of a

[12] S. J. Case, *Jesus: A New Biography* (Chicago, 1927), pp. 391 ff.

PAUL THE JEW 165

position similar to the one he advocated in Corinth where the matter was localized in the question of eating meat offered in pagan sacrifice. Here the situation is much more general, representing an ascetic tendency. The Pauline principle enunciated is the same, the curbing of Christian liberty because of the scrupulousness of the "weak." Christian love should take precedence over Christian liberty, but the circumstances leading to the articulation of that principle are different.

This ascetic tendency was not limited to the Christian community in Rome. It was part of the general *zeitgeist*. Judaism on the whole was unascetic, but there were the Essenes, John the Baptist, and the Therapeutae, the sect in Egypt, all of which attest the presence of asceticism, even in Judaism. The Jew would not consider the observance of his ceremonial law an ascetic measure. In the question of asceticism much hinges on definition. Paul is ascetic in some respects and extremely unascetic in others. Most of the phases of Paul's asceticism have been treated in other connections, i.e., his hardships willingly endured, even rejoiced in (II Cor. 11:24-30), his readiness for martyrdom (Phil. 2:17), his contest with Satan (II Cor. 12:7), his attitude towards marriage (I Cor. 7).

Romans, chapter 14 is very un-Jewish. Here are some of the most advanced views on "days" and "diet" to be found in the New Testament. No normal Jew would say, "I know and I am convinced that nothing is unclean in itself; only to the person who regards it so is it unclean" (14:14). Or "One man thinks one day above another, while another man thinks every day the same. Let each one be fully assured in his own mind" (14:5). These utterances fly straight in the face of the Sabbath laws and the levitical legislation regarding diet. We may approve "anything that does not proceed from conviction is wrong," but the Jew could not in the above mentioned cases.

There is no method of harmonization of Paul's expressed attitudes on Jews and Judaism. The point of view of the present writer is to take Paul in his social situation and see what he does and what he says that has bearing on ethical problems. Where there is conflict between behavior and ideas, the practice is treated as normative for Paul's ethical outlook. According to this method we take Paul as he *does*, bring whatever facts we can into that picture, and try to account for those that must remain outside.

Although Paul (like Philo) may have thought himself a perfectly good Jew, his definition of that type of person would not have suited any thorough-going Jew of Palestine or of the Diaspora. To be sure he makes constant appeal to Scripture, but the fact remains that Paul behaved in most un-Jewish fashion, and the Jews as a whole rejected the new preaching. This is no cause for surprise, for Paul's thoroughgoing spiritism put his interpretation outside the pale of Judaism. He insisted that the new movement waive circumcision for Gentiles; he practised table-fellowship with Gentiles at Antioch; he did not observe the Sabbath and dietary laws. A Jew would have been scandalized at a meeting of Corinthian Christians when they were in full "spiritual" mettle, and no one could blame him!

His attitude toward Jews as we see it in his letters is always conditioned by circumstances. Paul would not need to tell us that he aimed to be all things to all men. Nothing is clearer. When he finds himself, back to the wall, fighting for what he considers of the utmost importance, he treats Jew and Gentile alike. There is really not much choice in the way Paul treats an enemy, whether he be the

PAUL THE JEW 167

conceited Corinthian, the Jew attempting to stir up trouble for him, or the Judaising Christian acting from convictions as deep as his own. But when Paul wants to be diplomatic, whether in the interests of the collection for Jerusalem Christians or in the interest of conciliating his fellow-countrymen, he can be just the opposite from what he is most of the time when he is not striving for diplomacy.

If we regard Romans as being like any other letter, it blurs the picture of Paul that stands out pretty vividly; but if we do our discounting on this letter we keep our picture of Paul consistent with itself, and the problem remains to account for this letter. It seems to the present writer that it is a studied attempt without exclusive bearing on Rome, to unite the Christian forces, conciliate the Jews, explain calmly what his gospel is (hence the spiritism in the letter) and perhaps enlist the non-Pauline but important Roman church for his projected evangelization of Spain. After all, is there any real reason why we should take this letter, where Paul is unquestionably trying to put his best foot foremost, so to speak, and rate it above those letters which depict Paul in a real and living situation? We need not discount Paul's feeling of grief at seeing the Jews pass by the new movement, even persecute it, when they ought to be seeing God's method of salvation as he sees it, which he would say is the true Jewish way, according to the Scriptures!

What must be protested in the light of an inductive study of Paul is that Paul's ethics is sufficiently and satisfactorily explained out of Judaism alone. This does not mean that the influence of Paul's Jewish heritage was slight in this area. The interest of Judaism in ethics is certain, as was the interest also of Stoicism. But what seems increasingly clear is that Paul's ethical judgments were much more conditioned by the contemporary social situation than they were conditioned by any heritage from his past. A study of Paul's temperament throws more light on his ethical outlook than does a survey of Jewish ethical emphases. His conviction that the end of the world was just around the corner did more to shape his judgment on marriage than did his Jewish heritage. Nothing could be further from the Jewish ideal than Paul's attitude toward marriage. One needs no more than put the question of how much his judgment on the matter of circumcision of Gentiles was conditioned by the fact that he was nurtured in Judaism.

Moreover Paul's own insistence that ethical action is conditioned by the possession of the Spirit, that natural man cannot achieve a worthy ethical life, points away from Judaism as the norm of Paul's judgment. Judaism never based its ethics in mysticism; Paul does. Paul may respect the ethical standards of his ancestral faith; those standards cannot be achieved without the addition of a supernatural element, the Spirit. In the light both of Paul's actions and of his expressed basing of those actions in his new religious emphases, we may not subsume the whole question of the ethics of Paul under the general statement that he was a Jew and think that we have said the last word.

CONCLUSION

THE present study has sought to approach Paul and his teaching by way of his social experience. The critical situations which he met have been analyzed with a view to determining his sanctions for conduct, his modes of meeting human problems, his own behavior and his defense of that behavior where need for defense arose. The predominance of practical problems, which this angle of approach reveals, shows that Paul has been greatly over-estimated as an intellectual, particularly as the important early Christian theologian.

Practice was uppermost with Paul. The controversy over circumcision arose from Paul's practice of admitting Gentiles into the Christian family of the faith without circumcision. Necessity dictated this concession if Christianity were to be anything more than a movement comparable to proselyting for Judaism. Gentiles would not join the Jewish race in order to become Christians. Paul did not demand the impossible. When conflict arose later he justified his action by appeal to experience. These uncircumcised Gentiles had the "Spirit" *(pneuma)*, that divine essence which Paul had come to believe was the prime requisite for every Christian. This new aspect of Paul's religion shifts the emphasis from Law observance as a means of salvation to spirit-possession as the norm of man's hope in the future or worthy ethical life in the present. A major tenet of Paul's religion was life *en*

Christō or *en kuriō*. Man must become a *new creation in Christ Jesus*. There is no other way. The fruits of the spirit are certain qualities of character, prized also in Judaism and in Stoicism, but not achieved through the intervention of any supernatural strength or agency.

The immediate basis in the experience of Paul for this new and thoroughly un-Jewish type of religious experience is his conversion and consequent transfer of loyalty. Such experiences are not so sudden as they appear. If Paul had been finding the normal satisfactions in his ancestral faith he would not have made this transfer of loyalty. Most Jews did not. The Christian movement became predominantly Gentile even at an early date in its history. The strong individualism and emotionalism, as evidenced in Paul's letters, point to a Gentile type of religious experience. Modern research has demonstrated the affinity of the Pauline presentation of religion to that of the contemporary mystery cults. This approach satisfied the cravings of Paul's emotional nature as Judaism had not been able to do. Once the transfer was made, Paul, who never did things by halves, became just as devoted to the new faith as he had been to the old. He is an example of the temperament that is constitutionally unable to see its own mistakes. He is always gloriously right, whether it is as a fanatical Jew ready to persecute those who see another way or whether it is as a fanatical Christian amazed that the Jews turn away from the true Jewish message, which but for their blindness they would see.

The Corinthian correspondence reveals a variety of social situations ranging from the problems of morals and marriage to those of dress and behavior appropriate to Christian women who attend the cult meetings, or from

CONCLUSION 171

the attitude proper to the slave to the correct observance of the Lord's Supper. Paul's judgment on the matter of marriage reveals a different norm for each different type of situation. Circumstances rule. Paul often rationalizes his decision by appeal to *spiritism*. Other appeals are to the appearance of the Lord *(Parousia)* and to tradition, with an occasional appeal to social experience, as in the case of the immoral man whom he likens to leaven which must be purged out of the community. The extent to which Christians might participate in pagan social and religious life was a burning issue in Corinth. Paul appeals to the motive of brother-love and consideration for the weak Christian, but his clinching argument is the appeal to spiritism as he points out the disasters attendant upon improper observance of the Eucharist, and vouches for the reality of the demon behind the pagan's idol.

The great variety of standards shows that Paul simply did the best he could in the immediate situation, and when conflict arose he attempted to justify his course of action or his judgment. His justifications do not always appeal to the modern mind as rational in spite of past efforts to see in Paul the profound intellectual leader of primitive Christianity.

Was Paul an intellectual? If so, he naturally links up with either Jewish or Gentile intellectualism of the first century. The one reference to Paul's alleged rabbinic training is found in the traditions of Acts, but Paul's silence on the subject at the points where speech would be expected leads us to leave that subject an open question, with the probabilities against it. He does not mention it in his famous catalogue of the advantages of Judaism which had been his, and undue modesty on his own apostolic credentials was not a Pauline characteristic. Gentile intellectualism of the first century is practically synonymous with Stoicism, and an inductive approach to this problem reveals whole areas in which there is no common ground; and on the issues where we have the judgments of both, Paul decidedly is not a Stoic intellectual. Philo, his Alexandrian contemporary, links much more closely with Stoicism than does Paul. The major Stoic emphases are utterly lacking in Paul's letters, and what he makes central in the exposition of his faith is quite outside the pale of Stoic intellectualism.

Not that Stoicism had no influence. It may be regarded as established that Paul had contacts with Stoicism in the area of practice rather than of theory. Paul is indebted to the Stoics in the area of technique and method— his method of preaching is like that of the Stoic street-preachers of his time. But with the life and thought of the intellectuals there seems to have been no contact. Paul does not meet living problems in the Stoic way. He used certain Stoic patterns of ethical teaching, notably the vice and virtue lists and the *haustafel* pattern. These were also employed by Hellenistic Judaism, but whatever the avenues of entrance into early Christianity the evidence of Paul's use of these Greek forms is clear.

The use of other traditional material in Paul's letters is also attested by the inductive approach to those letters. Paul acknowledges himself indebted to Christian tradition and to Christian practice (I Cor. 15:1-11; I Cor. 11:16). Every letter reveals his firm belief in the *Parousia*. On at least one occasion he was grateful for the approval of the pillar apostles in Jerusalem (Gal. 2:1 ff.). There is also an ever-present Jewish element in his letters, finding expression largely in his idea of God, the Pharisaic doctrine of the resurrection, and the appeal to Scripture. It should be noted that this is in the area of intellectual content, not in the area of practice, or of the majority of his expressed attitudes on Jews and Judaism. Only by the elevation of the letter to the Romans above the other letters of Paul, have writers been able to picture him as sympathetic to the Jewish outlook.

Paul's concern for ethics can be derived more directly from his Jewish than from his pagan environment. Judaism did not separate religion and ethics; neither did Paul. In the Greek world ethical teaching was the concern of the philosophers and the Stoic contribution in this field reached the common people through the Cynic-Stoic preachers. It is obviously impossible to evaluate accurately the respective contributions of each part of his environment. Paul was a Hellenistic Jew and as such was indirectly influenced by the Greek spirit, as well as directly influenced through the impact of pagan preaching as he heard it on the street corners of Tarsus as a youth, and in other cities as a Christian missionary.

But his social experience was the major factor in determining his ethical judgments, as a careful study of the crises which he handled abundantly attests. Many of his problems could not be settled by any appeal to the past. He had to be content with compromise at times. He had to take people as he found them and appeal to whatever incentives to more worthy living he could find. As his immediate judgments on ethical matters were conditioned by the necessity of circumstances, so also the presence of collections of ethical precepts in his letters was motivated by the needs of his communities. The use of traditional material and the dependence on Stoic and Hellenistic-Jewish moral appeals is attested. Originality in the formulation of ethical precepts is the last thing to be expected of any religious or ethical teacher. Moral codes and moral teaching do not come in that way. It is certainly no loss to realize that Paul gratefully accepted and used moral appeals which had been found valuable in the struggle against moral laxity by previous Christians, Jews, and Stoics. Experience, too, taught him the values inherent in the approach of the popular street-preachers of his world and the vital significance of the emotional appeal of the mystery cults.

Only to those who insist that Paul sponsors modern attitudes will these conclusions be unwelcome. Little by little Paul has been put back into the first century and related to its life and problems. It has long been recognized that Paul labored under the impression that the end of the world was imminent, and that this conviction conditioned some of his teaching about marriage. We do not hold Paul's eschatological outlook today. In the organization of Christian worship we should be very loath to use any Pauline church as a criterion in the light of what we know about spiritistic behavior. Similarly the modern mind finds the spiritistic basis of the motivation of ethical conduct equally untenable. *Spirit* is filled with an entirely new content, and such reinterpretation of Pauline phraseology is inevitable; but the fact to remember is that Paul did not see in the term its modern connotation. To him it was not something conveniently general, but disturbingly concrete.

Romans, chapter 12 will still be a good manual of Christian instruction regardless of its spiritistic introduction or its use of the diatribe form. Consideration for the weak brother will still characterize Christian ethical teaching, nor is Paul's insistence upon the supremacy of love among the Christian virtues likely to be outgrown. The life

Paul lived among the Thessalonians *for their good* will still command admiration, and the hardships which he willingly endured out of loyalty to Christ will still inspire devotion. The weaknesses of the very human Paul will not be glossed over, but the picture will be one of light and shade with the probable adherence to that beautiful bit of advice that Paul once offered to the Philippians, "Finally brothers, think constantly about the things that are true, venerable, righteous, pure, pleasing, gracious: things that are excellent and worthy of praise."

BIBLIOGRAPHY

Chapter I

Burton, E. D. *The Epistle to the Galatians.* New York, 1920. Introd. pp. xxi-xliv discusses what constituted Galatia.

Case, S. J. *Experience With the Supernatural in Early Christian Times.* New York, 1929.

——— *The Social Origins of Christianity.* Chicago, 1923.

Cumont, Franz. *Astrology and Religion Among the Greeks and Romans.* New York, 1912.

——— *Oriental Religions in Roman Paganism.* Chicago, 1911 (3rd German ed., Leipzig, 1931).

Dibelius, M. *An Die Thessaloniker I/II An Die Philipper.* Tübingen, 1925.

Jackson, F. J. F., and Lake, K. *The Beginnings of Christianity,* Vol. I. London, 1920.

Lietzmann, Hans. *An Die Galater.* Tübingen, 1923.

Lohmeyer, Ernst. *Der Brief an die Philipper.* Göttingen, 1928.

Lütgert, D. W. *Gesetz und Geist.* Gütersloh, 1919.

Ropes, J. H. *The Singular Problem of the Epistle to the Galatians.* Cambridge, 1929.

——— "The Epistle to the Romans and Jewish Christianity," *Studies in Early Christianity* (ed., S. J. Case), New York, 1928.

Weidinger, Karl. *Die Haustafeln.* Leipzig, 1928.

Wendland, Paul. *Die Hellenistisch-Römische Kultur.* Tübingen, 1912.

Chapter II

Gardner, Percy. *The Religious Experience of St. Paul.* London, 1911.

BIBLIOGRAPHY

Lietzmann, Hans. *An Die Korinther I/II*. Tübingen, 1931.
Morgan, William. *The Religion and Theology of Paul*. Edinburgh, 1917.
Reitzenstein, Richard. *Die Hellenistischen Mysterien-religionen*. Leipzig, 1927.
Schweitzer, Albert. *Die Mystik des Apostel Paulus*. Tübingen, 1930. English translation, *The Mysticism of Paul the Apostle*. New York, 1932.
Von Soden, Hans. *Sacrament und Ethik bei Paulus*. Marburg, 1931.
Weiss, Johannes. *Der Erste Korintherbrief*. Göttingen, 1910.
Willoughby, H. R. *Pagan Regeneration*. Chicago, 1929.
Windisch, Hans. *Der Zweite Korintherbrief*. Göttingen, 1920.
Wrede, William. *Paul*. Tübingen, 1904.

Chapter III

Angus, Samuel A. *The Mystery Religions and Christianity*. New York, 1925.
Cumont, F. *Oriental Religions in Roman Paganism*. Chicago, 1911 (3rd German ed., Leipzig, 1931).
Deissmann, Adolf. *Paul: A Study in Social and Religious History*. 2nd Eng., ed., New York, 1926.
Hatch, Edwin. *Influence of Greek Ideas upon the Christian Church*. London, 1891.
Lake, Kirsopp. *Landmarks in the History of Early Christianity*. London, 1922.
Lietzmann, Hans. *An Die Korinther I/II*. Tübingen, 1931.
Moore, G. F. *Judaism*. 2 vols. Cambridge, 1927.
Reitzenstein, R. *Die Hellenistischen Mysterien-religionen*. Leipzig, 1927.
Weiss, Johannes. *Der Erste Korintherbrief*. Göttingen, 1910. See Introd., pp. vii-xxxvi, for an excellent brief account of Corinth and her people.

Chapter IV

Arnold, E. V. *Roman Stoicism*. Cambridge, 1911.
Bevan, Edwyn. *Stoics and Skeptics*, pp. 85-114. Oxford, 1913.

Böhlig, Hans. *Die Geisteskultur von Tarsos.* Göttingen, 1913.
Bonhöffer, Adolf. *Epiktet und das Neue Testament,* pp. 98-180. Giessen, 1911.
Bultmann, Rudolf. *Der Stil der Paulinischen Predigt,* pp. 107-109. Göttingen, 1910.
Chappuis, Paul. *La Destinée de L'Homme,* pp. 34-51. Paris, 1926.
Cumont, Franz. *Oriental Religions in Roman Paganism,* Ch. VII. Chicago, 1911.
——— *Astrology and Religion Among the Greeks and Romans.* New York, 1912.
De Faye, Eugene. *St. Paul,* pp. 103-105. Paris, 1929.
Dibelius, M. *An Die Kolosser, Epheser, Philemon.* Tübingen, 1927.
——— *An Die Philipper.* Tübingen, 1925.
Emerson, R. W. *Plutarch's Moralia,* Introd. pp. xi-xiii. Ed., W. W. Goodwin, Boston, 1870.
Lietzmann, Hans. *An Die Römer.* Tübingen, 1928.
Lightfoot, J. B. "St. Paul and Seneca," *St. Paul's Epistle to the Philippians.* Cambridge, 1868; London, 1908.
Lohmeyer, Ernst. *Die Briefe an die Kolosser und an Philemon.* Göttingen, 1930.
Mahaffy, J. P. *The Greek World under Roman Sway.* London, 1890.
Murray, Gilbert. *Five Stages of Greek Religion.* Oxford, 1925.
Reitzenstein, R. *Die Hellenistischen Mysterien-religionen.* Leipzig, 1927.
Rose, H. J. *The Roman Questions of Plutarch.* Oxford, 1924.
Scott, Walter. *Hermetica.* Oxford, 1924.
Toussaint, C. *L'Hellenisme et L'Apôtre Paul.* Paris, 1921.
Weidinger, Karl. *Die Haustafeln,* pp. 40-50. Leipzig, 1928.
Wendland, Paul. *Die Hellenistisch-Römische Kultur,* pp. 75-96. Tübingen, 1912.

Chapter V

Böhlig, Hans. *Die Geisteskultur von Tarsos,* pp. 84-88, 131-134, 163-166. Göttingen, 1913.

BIBLIOGRAPHY

Bosworth, E. I. *Romans*. New York, 1919.
Bousset, W. *Die Religion des Judentums*. Tübingen, 1926.
Causse, A. *Les Disperses D'Israel*, pp. 130-160. Paris, 1929.
Enslin, M. S. *The Ethics of Paul*. New York, 1930.
Kummel, W. G. *Römer 7 und die Bekehrung des Paulus*. Leipzig, 1929.
Lake, Kirsopp. *The Earlier Epistles of Paul*. London, 1911.
Moore, G. F. *Judaism*. 2 vols. Cambridge, 1927.
Ropes, J. H. "The Epistle to the Romans and Jewish Christianity," *Studies in Early Christianity* (ed., S. J. Case). New York, 1928.

INDEX

ABRAHAM, 30; acquitted by faith, 153.
Against Apion, Josephus, 15.
Against Heresies, Irenaeus, 122.
Alexander, 103, 139.
Alexandria, 97; Judaism of, 138.
Anglican Theological Review, The, 9 n., 17 n.
Annals, Tacitus, 85 n.
Antioch, 9; Christian practice in, 17, 37, 144, 166.
Antiquities, Josephus, 139 n.
Antisthenes, 89; founder of Cynicism, 103.
Antoninus, Marcus Aurelius, 103, 118 n.
Apocrypha and Pseudepigrapha of the Old Testament, ed. R. H. Charles, 96 n.
Apollos, 41, 45, 51.
Aristotle, 103, 104, 106.
Arnold, E. V., 109, 109 n., 177.
Astrology and Religion Among the Greeks and Romans, Cumont, 106 n., 178.

BARNABAS, 14, 16-17.
Barth, Karl, 3.
Bevan, Edwyn, 105, 177.
Bion, 129.
Böhlig, Hans, 104, 111, 111 n., 112; on Tarsus and Tarsian Judaism, 138-42, 138 n.; on *Romans*, 13, 164, 178.
Bonnöffer, Adolf, 178; on relation of Paul to Stoicism, 110-12.
Bosworth, E. I., 152 n., 179.
Bultmann, Rudolf, 111, 111 n., 112, 178.
Burton, E. D., 25 n., 26 n., 176.

CALIGULA, 15.
Carlyon, James, 123 n.
Case, S. J., 164 n., 176.
Chappuis, Paul, 112-13, 112 n., 178.
Charles, R. H., 96 n.
Christ, Jesus, 23-24, 28, 34, 108; Cross of, 60-62, 120-24, 153; party of, 41.
Christians, 5, 22-23, 135, 151; in Colossae, 108; in Corinth, 62, 69-73, 89-91, 147; in Galatia, 19-21; persecution of, 10, 12-13, 19-20; in Philippi, 12-13, 34-35, 51, 54, 58; in Rome, 161-62; in Thessalonica, 12, 53-54; "weak," 90-91, 165.
Cicero, 103, 105, 108, 119, 125 n., 128, 134; on the attitude of the Romans toward the Jews, 14.
Cities of St. Paul, The, Ramsay, 138 n.
Clement I, to the Corinthians, 47-48.
Clement of Alexandria, 89 n.
Colossae, ascetic practices in, 108; astrological speculation in, 124-25; syncretism in, 107-08.
Colossians, 62, 122; the *haustafel* in, 131-32.
Colwell, Ernest C., 17 n.
Conjugal Precepts, Plutarch, 116.
Consolatory Letter to His Wife, Plutarch, 117.
Corinth, 11-12, 39; antinomianism in, 43-46, 62, 72-74, 77, 81, 162; asceticism in, 72, 81, 86; Christians in, 40-45, 56, 71-73; eating meat offered in pagan sacrifice in, 70, 98-92; Gnosticism in, 62, 89 ff.; Christian meetings in, 64 ff., 98 ff.; women in, 52, 67, 93-98, 170-71.
Corinthians I, II, 53, 125, 149-50; analysis of, 46-48; antinomianism in,

43-46, 72 ff., 75; marriage and divorce in, 79 ff.; problems treated in, 39-40, 69; slavery in, 87-88.
Cumont, Franz, 70, 70 n., 105, 105 n., 176-78.
Cyprian, 85, 85 n.

DAMASCUS, 11, 48.
De Finibus, Cicero, 121, 121 n.
De Officiis, Cicero, 125 n.
Deissmann, Adolf, 3, 25 n., 177.
Destinee de L'Homme, La, Chappuis, 112 n., 178.
Dibelius, Martin, 128, 176, 178.
Dio Chrysostom, 138-39.
Diogenes, 103, 129.
Discourses, Epictetus, notes on, 76, 81, 87, 119, 120, 126, 130.
Dress of Virgins, On the, Cyprian, 85 n.

EARLIER *Epistles of Paul, The*, Lake, 150 n., 179.
Ecclesiasticus, Sirach, 95-96, 127, 136.
Emerson, R. W., 114-15.
Encyclopaedia of Religion and Ethics, Hastings, 89 n.
Enslin, M. S., 5-6, 135 n., 147 n., 179.
Epaphroditus, 54, 58.
Epictetus, 103, 108, 110, 114, 119, 120 n., 126 n., 130, 134; on adultery, 75-76; on asceticism, 118; on marriage, 80-81; on slavery, 87, 87 n.
Epicureanism, 70, 103, 107.
Epiktet und das Neue Testament, Bonhöffer, 110, 178.
Epistle 5, Seneca, 118 n.
Epistle 12, Seneca, 131 n.
Epistle 40, Seneca, 125 n.
Epistle 41, Seneca, 119 n.
Epistle 52, Seneca, 130 n.
Epistle 65, Seneca, 118 n.
Epistle 94, Seneca, 116 n.
Erster Korintherbrief, Der, Weiss, 94 n., 95 n., 177.
Essenes, 165; Philo on, 97.
Ezra, III, 141.

FIRMNESS *of the Wise Man, On the*, Seneca, 116 n., 126 n.
Five Stages of Greek Religion, Murray, 107 n., 178.
"Fleisch und Die Sünde, Das," 156 n.
Formgeschichte, vii, 164.
Fragments, Philo, 97 n.

GALATIANS, antinomianism in, 31-32; astrological speculation in, 29-32; controversy over circumcision in, 19-21, 37; message and method of Paul in, 23-26, 119; *paraenesis* in, 73; repudiation of the Law in, 28-31; and *Romans*, 149-50; use of Scripture by Paul in, 29-31, 143.
Gamaliel, 140, 147, 147 n.
Geistes-kultur von Tarsos, Die, Böhlig, 104-05, 111 n., 138 n., 178-79.
Gnosticism, 62, 108; in Corinth, 43-45, 88-89, 99-100; religion, not philosophy, 121; terminology of, 26, 44, 66, 72-74, 121-24, 156.
Goodspeed, Edgar Johnson, 85 n.
Greek World Under Roman Sway, The, Mahaffy, 114 n., 178.

HANDBUCH *zum Neuen Testament*, 127.
Hatch, Edwin, 71 n., 177
Haustafeln, Die, Weidinger, 7, 176, 178.
Heitmüller, W., 11 n.
Hellenism, 4, 102, 136, 139.
Hellenistischen Mysterien—religionen, Die, Reitzenstein, 25 n., 44, 66 n., 101 n., 177, 178.
Hellenistisch-Römische Kultur, Die, Wendland, 104 n., 121 n., 130 n., 176, 178.
Hermetica, 105.
Hillel, 140.

INFLUENCE *of Greek Ideas upon the Christian Church, The*, Hatch, 71 n., 177.
Irenaeus, 122.

INDEX

JAMES, 11, 16.
Jerusalem, 14; early Christianity in, 10-11; Judaisers from, 20; visit of Paul to, 16-17.
Jesus, 108; death of, 144; Judaism of, 135; Paul's appeal to, 82; religion of in Paul, 101; resurrection of, 142; teaching of, 163.
Jesus: A New Biography, Case, 164 n.
Jewish-Christians, 9, 9 n., 20.
Jewish People in the Time of Jesus Christ, The, Schürer, 15 n.
Jews, 89, 135, 138 n., 165, 170; advantages of, 146-47; attitude of Paul toward in *Romans*, 149, 152-53, 159-61, 166-67; attitude of Romans toward, 14-15; of the Diaspora, 146; divorce among, 83; ideas of about women, 96-98; in Jerusalem, 10; in Tarsus, 139-42; and their traditions, 147-49.
John the Baptist, 165.
John of Stobi, 130.
Josephus, 15, 139, 139 n., 146.
Journal of Biblical Literature, 134 n.
Journal of Religion, 147 n.
Judaism, Moore, notes on, 94, 136, 137.
Judaism, 22, 37, 48, 60, 66, 101, 109-10, 143, 154, 156; advantages of, 27; appeal of, to Gentiles, 14; asceticism in, 165 ff.; attitude of toward women, 94-98; complexity of, 135-36; ethical sensitivity in, 70-71, 73; Hellenistic (i. e., Diaspora), 128, 130, 132-33, 136-38, 140-41, 152, 164, 172; of Palestine, 139-40; relation of Paul to, 145-49, 159-62, 166, 173; of Tarsus, 111, 140; salvation in, 25; use of curse in, 74.
Judgment, 28, 63; acquittal in the, 120, 143, 153-54, 159; "justification by faith" in the, 18, 25 n.

KORINTHER, I. II., *An Die*, Lietzmann, 41 n., 177.

LAKE, K., 72, 150 n., 176, 177, 179.
Law of Moses, 5, 20, 114, 128, 145-46; appeal of Paul to, 28-31; attitude of Paul toward in *Romans*, 151-56, 161; Jews and the, 147-49, 168; relation of Paul to the, 155-57; repudiation of by Paul, 28-31; superseded by Christ, 60; unnecessary for Christians, 21, 25, 38, 143, 159.
Lietzmann, Hans, 100, 127, 176, 177, 178; notes on, 41, 127, 156.
Lightfoot, J. B., 109, 109 n., 126, 178.
Lohmeyer, Ernst, 13, 176, 178.
Lütgert, W., 19, 31, 151.

MAHAFFY, J. P., 114, 114 n., 178.
Meditations, Marcus Aurelius, 118 n.
Messiah, 9, 13, 22.
Messianism, in early Christianity, 22-23.
Minor Dialogues, Seneca, 116 n.
Moore, G. F., 179; notes on, 94, 135, 136, 137.
Moralae Epistulae, Seneca, 87 n.
Moses, 15, 60, 128.
Murray, Gilbert, 107, 107 n., 157, 178.
Musonius, 130.
Mysteries, 23-24, 119, 170, 174; of Cybele-Attis, 23, 32; of Isis, 89; of Mithra, 143; Orphic, 118; terminology of in Paul, 27-28, 43-44, 54, 62-67, 73, 74, 77, 84, 86, 93-94, 98-99, 120-24, 126, 170.

NEO-PLATONISM, 70, 104, 114.
Neo-Pythagoreans, 104, 118, 130.
New Testament Word Studies, Burton, 25 n.

ORIENTAL *Religions in Roman Paganism*, Cumont, 70 n., 105 n., 176, 177, 178.

PAUL, allegory in writings of, 30, 143; Apocalyptic imagery in writings of, 22-23, 26-27, 33, 35-36, 40, 54,

63, 72, 74, 80, 113-14, 123-24, 132, 142-44, 171-72; attitude of toward circumcision, 15-16, 17-18, 20-21, 37, 123, 143-46; belief of in demons, 74, 84, 91-92; conversion of, 11, 147; diatribe style of, 110-11, 133, 162, 174; dualism in writings of, 35, 72; early Christian message of, 13, 22-23; eschatology of, 4, 23; imprisonment of, 13, 151; influence of Stoicism on, 109, 112, 134; on Judgment, 63-64; on marriage, 32, 79-86; the missionary, 3-4, 10, 113, 173; motivation of conduct in writings of, 35, 76-78; mysticism of, 4, 26-28, 35-36, 38, 60-63, 64-67, 72, 84-86, 120, 123-25, 157; neglect of ethics of, 3-4; *paraenesis* in writings of, 6-8, 31-32, 37, 46, 162; personal characteristics of, 37-38, 44, 48-59, 148 ff., 168; relation of to Gentile intellectualism, 102-34; religion of, 21-31, 59-68, 120-21; on resurrection, 23, 34-35, 61, 63, 114, 124, 142, 172; sacraments in writings of, 39, 42, 69-70, 89-93, 98, 114, 171; on slavery, 87-88; social approach to, 4-5, 18; sources of the ethics of, 167-68; Spirit and *Pneuma* in writings of, 16, 24-27, 26 n., 35-36, 50, 60-64, 66-67, 72, 74-75, 77-78, 81, 84-85, 92, 119-20, 122-25, 151, 168-69; the theologian, 3-4, 24, 169; world-view of, 140-143. See Judaism; Law of Moses.
"Paul and Gamaliel," 147.
Paul and the Gnostic Quest, Carlyon, 123 n.
"Paul and Seneca," Lightfoot, 109 n.
Paul: A Study in Social and Religious History, Deissmann, 25 n., 177.
Pearson, A. C., 89 n.
Peter, 10-11, 16-17, 28.
Philo, 101 n., 104-05, 128, 143, 156, 166; on marriage and women, 96-97; on the Roman attitude toward the Jews, 15, 15 n.; relation of to Stoicism, 134, 134 n., 136-37, 137 n., 172.
Pirke Aboth, 96 n.
Plato and Platonism, 103-04, 117.
Plutarch, 105, 108, 119, 134; *Conjugal Precepts*, 116-17; the gentleman of culture, 114-15; as priest of Pythian Apollo, 118.
Posidonius, 104-06, 111, 156.
Pro Flacco, Cicero, 14 n.
Pythagoreans, 105.

QUESTIONS *and Solutions*, Philo, 97 n.

RAMSAY, Sir William, 138 n.
Reitzenstein, Richard, 25 n., 26, 26 n., 44, 66 n., 100, 101 n., 119, 121, 122 n., 177, 178.
Riddle, Donald W., 9 n.
Römer, An Die, Lietzmann, 127 n., 156 n., 178.
Roman Questions of Plutarch, The, Rose, 115 n., 178.
Romans, analysis of, 151-59; attitude toward Jews and Judaism in, 159-61, 173; Lütgert and Ropes on, 20; occasion of, 149-51.
Romans, Bosworth, 152 n., 179.
Roman Stoicism, Arnold, 109 n., 177.
Ropes, J. H., 176, 179; on the Judaistic controversy, 151; on the "radicals," 19-20, 32.
Rose, H. J., 115, 115 n.

ST. *Paul's Epistle to the Philippians*, Lightfoot, 109 n.
Satan, 74, 165.
Schürer, E., 15 n.
Scriptures, 161; use of by Paul, 29-30, 38, 143-44, 153, 166, 172-73.
Seneca, 103, 114, 125, 128, 131, 134; notes on, 116, 118, 119, 125, 130, 131; on asceticism, 118; "God" and "Holy Spirit" in, 119; and Paul,

108-09; on popular philosophy, 130; on the sexes, 116; on slaves, 87.
Shammai, 83, 140.
Sirach, 95, 127, 136.
"So-called Jewish Christians, The," Riddle, 9 n.
Special Laws, On, Philo, 97 n.
Spirit, Soul and Flesh, Burton, 26 n.
Stephen, 10.
Stil der Paulinischen Predigt, Der, 111, 111 n., 178.
Stoicism, 25, 70, 143, 170; antecedents of, 102-04; astrology and fatalism in, 104-08; contribution of Posidonius to, 104-06; diatribe in, 129-30; the *haustafel* in, 127-28; interest of in ethics, 102-04, 167; mysticism in, 105; relation of to Paul, 108-13, 113-16, 119-21, 125-34, 172; on slavery, 87-88; vice and virtue catalogues in, 32, 35, 152.
"Stoic Strain in Christianity, The," Arnold, 109 n.
Strabo, 15, 89, 89 n.
Stromateis, Clement of Alexander, 89 n.

TARSUS, Böhlig's study of, 138-142, 138 n.; founded by Seleucus I, 139; refounded by Antiochus IV, 139;
Judaism of, 111, 111 n., 135, 146; street-preachers of, 130, 133-34, 173.
Tertullian, 85, 85 n.
Therapeutae, 165.
Thessalonians I, II, 149; *paraenesis* in, 33, 128.
Timothy, 12, 50.
Titus, 14, 16, 53, 59, 143.
Torah, The, 146, 148, 157.

VEILING of Virgins, On the, Tertullian, 85 n.
Virtue and Office of Ambassadors, On the, Philo, 15 n.

WEIDINGER, Karl, 7, 127, 132, 162, 176, 178.
Weiss, Johannes, 94, 94 n., 177.
Wendland, Paul, 104, 121, 129, 131, 176, 178; notes on, 104, 121, 130.
Willoughby, H. R., 25 n., 177.
Wisdom of Solomon, 152.

XENOPHON, 117.

ZEITSCHRIFT *für die neutestamentliche Wissenschaft,* 11 n.
"Zum Problem Paulus und Jesus," 11 n.

www.ingramcontent.com/pod-product-compliance
Lightning Source LLC
Chambersburg PA
CBHW030112010526
44116CB00005B/210